Dominican
Republic

Front cover: An idyllic beach on the north coast

Right: A rhinoceros iguana

TOP 10 ATTRACTIONS

Lake Enriquillo • Lying well below sea level, this large lake supports an abundance of wildlife, including flocks of pink flamingos *(page 48)*

Beaches • Miles of glorious sandy beaches line the coast

Cabarete • Conditions here are ideal for windsurfing, and there is plenty more to do in this north coast town *(page 68)*

Wildlife • The country boasts a rich variety of flora and fauna, from tropical flowers and butterflies to reptiles such as the rhinoceros iguana, found in the Parque Nacional Jaragua *(page 47)*

Santo Domingo cathedral • The first cathedral built in the Americas once housed the bones of Columbus *(page 29)*

Jarabacoa • White-water rafting is one of several river sports on offer in the area *(pages 52 and 80)*

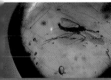
The Amber Museum • This Puerto Plata museum has some fascinating discoveries in store *(page 64)*

Pico Duarte • One of the most rewarding activities is a hike up the tallest peak in the Caribbean *(page 54)*

Los Haitises National Park • Known for its mangroves and distinctive limestone *mogotes* (pictured) *(page 73)*

The Fortaleza Ozama • The oldest fortress in the Americas is located in Santo Domingo *(page 26)*

CONTENTS

15

35

76

34

39

86

INTRODUCTION

Christopher Columbus landed on the island he later named Hispaniola during his first voyage to the New World in 1492. On his return to Spain he crumpled a piece of paper in his fist, released it and reported to the king and queen that it resembled the mountains of a paradise he had discovered. He wrote of the beauty of the rivers, shady palm trees, birds and flowers, going so far as to say that it surpassed all the rest of the world in beauty.

Still impressing visitors today with its lush tropical mountains and valleys, rushing rivers and miles of sandy beaches, the island of Hispaniola, lying among the Greater Antilles in the Caribbean, is in fact two countries with two distinct cultures and languages. The western third is occupied by French-speaking Haiti, while the eastern two thirds, or 48,442 sq km (18,704 sq miles), is the Spanish-speaking

Caribbean colours at Bayahibe

Dominican Republic. To the west of the island lie Jamaica and Cuba, to the east Puerto Rico and to the north the Bahamas and the Turks and Caicos Islands.

Landscape and Vegetation

The Dominican Republic is home to the two highest mountains in the Caribbean, the twin peaks of Pico Duarte and La Pelona, at 3,087m (10,127ft) and 3,082m (10,111ft) respectively, in the Cordillera Central mountain range.

Cacti thrive in the dunes at Las Calderas

Vegetation ranges from dry tropical forest in the west through subtropical humid forest on the slopes of the central mountains to pine forests at the summits. While arid areas are home to inhospitable acacia thorn bushes and cacti, wetter areas are overflowing with orchids, bromeliads, bougainvillea, ginger lilies and other exotic blooms. Palm trees are a feature of the landscape, Royal palms sprouting up in cattle pastures and coconuts along the coastline. Fruit trees are laden with tropical delights: mangoes, avocados, papaya, guava, while breakfast tables are weighed down with pineapple, passion fruit, melon and banana. Huge orchards of citrus and plantations of sugar cane and tobacco are found in the lowlands and rice paddies in the coastal flatlands, while at higher altitude strawberries, coffee and a wide range of vegetables are further proof of the country's fertility.

Climate

The temperature averages about 28°C (82°F) throughout the year. High up in the mountains frosts are occasionally registered at night, but elsewhere it rarely drops below 18°C (64°F) after dark. During the day it can rise to around 34°C (93°F), but sea breezes keep it comfortable on the coast. The first part of the year is usually the coolest, but then humidity picks up, often with heavy rains and localised flooding. Any time after June is hurricane season, with the worst hurricanes usually coming between September and November.

People

It is believed that at the time of Columbus' arrival, there were between 300,000 and 500,000 Amerindians, known as Taínos. They were hunter-gatherers living on fish, vegetables and fruit. The Spaniards referred to them all as 'Indians', believing that they had arrived in India, the aim of their voyage. Tragically, the Spanish enslaved the Taínos, tortured and murdered them and eliminated them as a race by the 1530s. African slaves were imported to replace the Taínos as a stronger and more reliable workforce and today the population of 8 million is largely a mixture of Spanish and African.

Dominicans are very colour conscious. Anyone who is black is assumed to come from Haiti, where a slave revolt was carried out at the end of the 18th century and the Africans drove out their white, French masters. Haitian rulers at one time controlled the whole of the island, and resentment against them

Uptown girls, Santo Domingo

Dominicans abroad

Well over a million Dominicans live abroad, about 1.3 million in the United States, where there is a large Dominican community in New York City. Some are illegal immigrants, but there is also a well-established resident population in the USA. Dominicans overseas are an important source of income: their remittances, estimated at some US$2.7 billion a year, keep many poor families afloat.

helped to instil colour discrimination in the people of what became the Dominican Republic after independence. There is a romantic attachment to the Amerindian heritage and people with fine features are often referred to as 'Indios', although it is highly unlikely that any of them can trace their ancestry back to Taíno blood. The elite is white and the paler your skin, the higher up the social ladder you will climb. Conversely, the poorest agricultural labourers are likely to be black Haitians.

Santo Domingo, the capital, is home to about half the population. The old colonial town, founded in 1498 and a World Heritage Site, now occupies only 1 percent of the total area of the city. Many of the most important buildings in the founding of the Americas are here, as it was from here that the conquistadores sailed to conquer other territories for Spain. It boasts the first cathedral, the first university and the first Audiencia Real (court) in the New World. Now, however, it is largely a site of tourist interest and most of the political and economic activity of the city takes place in the newer districts.

Income distribution is decidedly uneven. The growth of the city since the 1960s has attracted migrants from the countryside. Now they are packed into slum dwellings on the banks of the polluted river or on the outskirts of the city. Unemployment is rife, while drunkenness and drug abuse is common. A change of policy has led to greater spending in the countryside to reverse the trend, but it is a slow process.

Tourism and Attractions

The main engine of growth in the economy for the last 20 years has been tourism. The Dominican Republic has some of the best beaches in the world, with crystal clear water and plentiful sunshine. Large resort hotels have been widely embraced. However, this is also a place for the fit and active, the adventure seeker, the independent traveller who prefers a small, family-run hotel and the backpacker on a tight budget. Head inland into the mountains for river-rafting, canyoning, tubing and other adrenaline-pumping watersports. Take a few days to hike up Pico Duarte or go trekking elsewhere in the extensive National Parks. If your legs are up to it hire a mountain bike, one of the most rewarding ways of seeing the countryside.

Countryside near Constanza

Cabarete, on the north coast, is a major windsurfing centre, hosting international competitions. Kitesurfing has also taken off as another exciting sport. Underwater, the island has yet more to offer divers and snorkellers, with coral gardens, caves, pinnacles and wrecks providing a home for colourful fish and invertebrates. The largest visitors to Dominican waters, however, are the humpback whales, which migrate there from January to March, to mate and reproduce. Whale watching should not be missed if you are there at the right time.

A BRIEF HISTORY

The history of the Dominican Republic is well-documented after Columbus' arrival in 1492, but our knowledge of events prior to that is sketchy. Archaeological digs have unearthed settlements dating back almost 5,000 years, but there is no written record by the people who lived on the island. The first inhabitants were the Stone-Age Ciboneys, so called because of their word for stone *(ciba)* and man *(igney)*, who migrated there from what we now call Florida. Later arrivals came in several waves from Venezuela, the Taínos arriving in the 11th century and absorbing previous tribes.

The Arrival of Columbus

Christopher Columbus (Cristóbal Colón) landed on the north shore of the island he later named Hispaniola in 1492 with three small caravelles. He was trying to find a westerly route to Asia to trade in gold and spices and initially thought he had found India. He left a few men in charge of a settlement on the north coast and returned to Spain with some Taíno slaves and a few gold ornaments and jewellery. The Spanish Crown was delighted with the prospect of unlimited gold and ordered another voyage.

Statue of Columbus in Santo Domingo

Columbus' first settlement at La Isabela turned out to be a disaster and was wiped out by disease and Taíno attacks. His brother, Bartolomé, decided that the south coast was a healthier option and founded Santo Domingo on the east bank of the Ozama River in 1496. The Governor, Nicolás de Ovando, moved the town to the west bank in 1498, where he started to build houses made of stone rather than timber, and the first European city in the Americas was born. In 1509, Diego Colón, Christopher's son, took over the governorship and many of the city's oldest surviving structures date from this period. Santo Domingo welcomed many further explorers on their way from Spain to the Americas, and it became an important staging post for the conquistadores.

The colony's pre-eminence in the Spanish Crown was not to last, however, and it was soon overtaken by the richer jewels of Peru and Mexico. Although the Taínos were declared

Enriquillo, Freedom Fighter

Enriquillo, a Taíno who was baptised, has a special place in Dominican folklore as the first freedom fighter in Latin America. Fact and fiction became irrevocably entwined with the publication of a 19th-century romantic novel about him by Manuel de Jesús Galván. The story goes that Enriquillo, who married a Taíno woman, Mencía, in the Alcázar de Colón, became enraged when a nobleman, Andrés de Valenzuela, tried to rape his wife. He was whipped for complaining but took his case right up to the Audiencia Real. Failing to receive justice and threatened with imprisonment, he fled to the Sierra de Bahoruco where, with a guerrilla army of Taínos, he held out against Spanish forces. Eventually peace was negotiated by Hernando de San Martín and a treaty was signed by Carlos I of Spain, giving freedom and a reserve to the Taínos. However, Enriquillo did not live long, dying soon afterwards of one of the European diseases, possibly smallpox. Today, he is honoured with a lake named after him and a huge statue honouring his deeds stands at the junction of the road from Santo Domingo and the turn off to Lake Enriquillo.

free subjects of Spain in 1512, their population was completely wiped out by the 1530s as a result of Spanish brutality, slavery and disease and replaced as a workforce by African slaves. The city of Santo Domingo suffered from frequent hurricanes, an earthquake in 1562 and pirate attacks throughout the 16th and 17th centuries, so it was constantly struggling with rebuilding works.

Buccaneers

As soon as it became known that Spanish ships were carrying gold and silver back to Spain, the waters around the islands became infested with pirates. Eager to attack and capture the valuable cargo, the pirates' feats of derring-do soon became legendary. Some did not limit themselves to shipping and sacked towns in search of booty. One such privateer was Sir Francis Drake, who attacked Santo Domingo in 1586 from the landward side, where there were few defences. He looted and pillaged the city and once he'd stolen all he could, he burned it down, returning to England a national hero.

Sometimes the buccaneers varied their activities by attacking coastal shipping and sharing out the booty between them, but over time piracy around the island was stamped out and the buccaneers either became smallholders or joined other pirates in Jamaica.

Behind the name

Buccaneers were usually bands of escaped indentured labourers or slaves, who hid out in the hills surviving on hunting feral cattle and pigs. They smoked their catch over wood fires called *boucans*, which is how they got their name, and traded the meat and hides for guns and alcohol.

The Birth of Haiti

The French took advantage of Spain's lack of interest in maintaining its colony and invaded the western part of the island, establishing the French colony of Saint-Domingue, soon to become the largest sugar producer in the Caribbean. This colony lasted a century before the French Revolution and a fierce debate over slavery in France disrupted plantation life. In 1791 the slaves carried out the first and only successful slave rebellion, driving out their white, French masters. They called their new, independent country Haiti, meaning 'high ground' in the Taíno language. However, infighting between blacks and mulattos and frequent power struggles between ruthless leaders seriously damaged the economy and over the next 100 years Haiti slowly descended into poverty.

Defensive measure: Fortaleza de San Felipe at Puerto Plata

Santo Domingo meanwhile was an underpopulated backwater and easy prey for invaders. Between 1801 and 1809 the city was captured by Haiti, France, England and Spain, changing hands six times. In 1822–43 it was again under Haitian rule and during this unpopular regime fear and resentment of Haiti grew and the seeds of an independence movement were sown.

Independence Twice Over

On 27 February 1844 independence was achieved, while the three men who led the struggle against Haiti became national heroes: Juan Pablo Duarte, Francisco del Rosario Sánchez and Ramón Mella. They defeated Haitian troops in Santo Domingo and created the newly independent Dominican Republic, but were unable to hold together a government and the country was subject to frequent Haitian incursions. In November of that year, General Pedro Santana took over the government but was keen to negotiate a deal with a foreign power to become a protectorate. He finally achieved recolonisation with Spain, but the new arrangement was a complete failure. Spain's handling of the economy was

Juan Pablo Duarte, Father of the Nation

Wherever you go in the Dominican Republic, Calle Duarte is usually the main street in the town, Pico Duarte is the highest mountain in the island and Autopista Duarte is the main highway north from the capital. Duarte is everywhere, honoured as the instigator of independence from Haiti. Born in Santo Domingo in 1813, he was sent to Europe in 1828 to finish his studies. His travels through England, France and Spain influenced his thinking, and when he returned to his country in 1833 he developed the liberal ideas he had picked up into a nationalist policy against the Haitian occupation. He started a secret society called La Trinitaria, divided into groups of three, with each member recruiting three new members into the resistance network. The three leaders were Duarte, the lawyer Francisco del Rosario Sánchez, and the soldier Ramón Mella. Their first attempt at insurrection in 1843 was unsuccessful and a crackdown by troops forced Duarte into exile in Curaçao, while Sánchez went into hiding and Mella was arrested. There was further plotting and on 27 February 1844, Mella gave the signal for a second attempt. Haitian troops were defeated in Santo Domingo, a provisional junta was set up and the independent Dominican Republic was proclaimed. Duarte returned to a hero's welcome on 14 March. He became part of the junta, but was soon disillusioned with politics, the cynical manoeuvring and the power struggles, and quickly faded from the limelight.

disastrous and money was poured into keeping the peace when guerrillas took to the hills. Military repression was deeply resented and subsequent uprisings became known as the War of Restoration, which was brought to a close in 1865 when Spain finally gave up and evacuated all its troops and civil servants.

Bust of Duarte in Puerto Plata

US Intervention

The country remained impossible to govern with factionalism, economic weakness and Haitian invasions destabilising the new Republic. Governments came and went with remarkable speed as one strong man overthrew another, amassing fortunes while the country slid into bankruptcy. On several occasions Germany, being heavily involved in the tobacco trade, sent warships to collect debts. At this point the USA became anxious about German influence in the region and intervened, putting Dominican Customs into receivership in 1905.

Financial stability did not ensure political stability, however, and a succession of short-term presidencies, assassinations, uprisings and coups led the USA to bring in the Marines in 1916 and impose full military government. Although economically a success, with schools, sewers, roads and other infrastructure being built and the country becoming creditworthy, the occupying forces were deeply resented. Guerrilla warfare continued, exacerbated by land reform which dispossessed many peasant farmers, who took to the hills to fight. US troops were withdrawn in 1924.

The Trujillo Dictatorship

Elections in 1930 brought to the presidency the armed forces commander, Rafael Trujillo. Trujillo dominated the country for over 30 years and was one of the most feared and ruthless dictators ever seen in the Americas. Whether he or one of his puppets was president, it was Trujillo who controlled everything through his secret police, who operated with impunity, using torture, murder and blackmail to ensure loyalty. After a hurricane destroyed much of Santo Domingo in 1930, the megalomaniac Trujillo rebuilt the city and named it Ciudad Trujillo. In 1936 he renamed Pico Duarte, the tallest mountain in the Caribbean, Pico Trujillo.

Flag Monument in Santo Domingo

To Trujillo's credit, he modernised the country's infrastructure, repaid foreign debts, got rid of US control of Customs and introduced a national currency, the peso. However, he is chiefly remembered for his excesses and brutality. In 1937 around 10,000 Haitians in the Dominican Republic, mostly plantation workers, were rounded up and massacred. His racism led him to try and whiten the population by encouraging immigration from Europe and Japan while black Haitians were routinely abused and deported. Political opponents were regularly eliminated, but he finally overstepped the mark when in 1960 he plotted to assassinate the president of Venezuela, Rómulo Betancourt. The Organization of American States (OAS) imposed sanctions and pressure for change built up at home and abroad. In 1961, with CIA assistance, Trujillo was assassinated as he drove out of the capital to visit one of his mistresses.

Joaquín Balaguer

A Slow Start for Democracy

Joaquín Balaguer, president at the time, tried to hang on to power, as did the Trujillo family, but without success. Elections were held in 1962, which were won by the radical Juan Bosch, of the Partido Revolucionario Dominicano (PRD), formed in exile. His policies included land reform to redistribute estates confiscated by Trujillo and moves to combat unemployment and poverty, but despite an austerity programme to put order into the country's finances, he was greatly mistrusted by the oligarchy, the Church and the USA. Coming so soon after the 1959 Cuban revolution, any left wing leader in the region was doomed to failure and a military coup ousted him after only seven months.

A succession of governments failed to bring stability and as the country descended into civil war, the USA landed 23,000 troops in 1965, later backed by other forces from the OAS. Thousands of lives were lost before new elections were held in 1966. They were won by Balaguer, returned from exile at the head of his right wing Partido Reformista Social Cristiano (PRSC). Balaguer, who had been part of the Trujillo administration since 1930, went on to win elections in 1970,

Life goes on

1974, 1986, 1990 and 1994. The results were increasingly disputed until in 1994 his rival, José Franciso Peña Gómez of the PRD, alleged outright fraud. Balaguer was forced to hold new elections in 1996 in which he did not stand but succeeded in getting his candidate elected.

The 1980s and 1990s saw Dominicans endure extreme hardship, with poverty exacerbated by the world debt crisis. An IMF structural adjustment programme brought strikes and violence as high inflation, unemployment and corruption continued unabated. State utilities were in disarray, the sugar industry was bankrupt and spending on health and education was minimal. Nevertheless, Balaguer spent heavily on grandiose construction projects.

In 2000 Balaguer stood for election for the last time, aged 93, but Hipólito Mejía, of the PRD, was ultimately elected. Initial enthusiasm for the new president soon waned and by 2003 he was mistrusted by a large majority. A banking fraud scandal led to the collapse of several financial institutions and the value of the peso plummeted. This brought inflation and a spiralling budget deficit. As ordinary people struggled to cope, evidence mounted of corruption among the president's cronies. The May 2004 presidential elections were won by former president Leonel Fernández (PLD), who held office in 1996–2000. He immediately set about restoring order to the country's finances, implementing an IMF stabilisation programme and investing in infrastructure and tourism. Although his government was not free of corruption allegations, he won re-election in 2008 by a comfortable margin.

Historical Landmarks

1492 Arrival of Christopher Columbus en route to the Indies. Contact with Europeans is the beginning of the end for the indigenous Taínos.

1496 Founding of Santo Domingo, the first capital in the Caribbean, on the east bank of the Ozama River, moved in 1498 to the west bank.

1586 Sir Francis Drake sacks Santo Domingo, the first of many English and French pirates to attack in the 16th and 17th centuries.

1682 The island of Hispaniola is divided between France in the west and Spain in the east.

1801–09 Santo Domingo is captured six times by Haiti, France, Britain and lastly, Spain.

1822–43 The country is occupied by Haiti.

1844 Independence is proclaimed by the three founding fathers, Juan Pablo Duarte, Francisco del Rosario Sánchez and Ramón Mella.

1861 Reannexation to Spain.

1865 The War of Restoration successfully ejects the Spanish.

1905 The USA intervenes to restore financial order and takes over the country's Customs, but political stability remains elusive.

1916–24 The USA imposes full military government.

1930 Rafael Leonidas Trujillo Molina, armed forces commander, wins the presidential elections, beginning a dictatorship which lasts until his assassination in 1961.

1962 The left winger, Juan Bosch, wins the elections but is overthrown by a US-backed coup amid fears that the island will follow Cuba into communism.

1966 Joaquín Balaguer, a former president under Trujillo, wins the elections, going on to hold office seven times until his final defeat in 1996.

2000 The presidency is won by Hipólito Mejía. Balaguer dies in 2002.

2003 The collapse of several financial institutions plunges the country into its worst economic crisis in decades.

2004 Presidential elections won by Leonel Fernández of the Dominican Liberation Party.

2008 Fernández is re-elected with a comfortable majority.

WHERE TO GO

Although the Dominican Republic occupies only part of Hispaniola, it is still a large country and you would need three weeks to see it all comfortably. There are good highways north, east and west out of Santo Domingo, but it takes 4–5 hours to drive to the beach resorts in the east (205km/127 miles to Punta Cana), to Barahona (200km/124 miles) in the west and Puerto Plata (215km/134 miles) on the north coast.

Roads are not so good across country, particularly where there are mountains, so it is easier to return to Santo Domingo if you are travelling from the north coast to the east or west. New highways between Santo Domingo and Samaná have cut the journey between the towns from four hours to less than two. If you want to travel from Samaná to Barahona or Punta Cana you will need to allow several hours of driving to cover the 400km (250 miles) for either journey.

Depending on the length of your stay, you could allocate two or three days in the capital, a few days on the beach and a few more days up in the mountains, allowing time for excursions from your base.

SANTO DOMINGO

Around 4 million people live in Santo Domingo, the capital of the Dominican Republic, a sprawling, scruffy city fanning out from the River Ozama. Most of the growth has occurred since the 1960s. Prior to that the main districts were the colonial zone and, just to the west of it, Gazcue, considered the modern city with upper-middle-class villas. The wealthier areas of the city are now all west of the river,

The expansive Playa Grande on the north coast

Santo Domingo Cathedral, resting place of Christopher Columbus

while to the east growth in cheaper housing has been so strong in recent years that the area has been reclassified as the Province of Santo Domingo.

The western seaboard is outlined by the attractive seafront drive, formally called Avenida George Washington, but familiarly known as the Malecón. Several international hotels enjoy the sea view here and there are endless construction projects of high rise apartment and office blocks. The Malecón occupies a special place in the lives of Dominicans, as it is here that carnival parades are held, as well as the merengue festival and regular outdoor evening discos and festivities.

The main arteries of the city running west to east are the Avenida 27 de Febrero and the Avenida John F. Kennedy. State and private buses and route taxis *(públicos)* run frequently along these roads and those bisecting them. A metro system of 16 stations opened in 2008, revolutionising public transport.

Four bridges cross the river to link the two sides of the city but they are bottlenecks for busy traffic. Three are named after the national heroes, Duarte, Mella and Sánchez, but recently a fourth has been added, named Juan Bosch after the late left wing politician who struggled for nearly four decades against the powers that be. The cruise ship port is at the mouth of the river with two separate piers. The Sans Souci yacht harbour has been completely redeveloped to take the largest cruise ships at the Don Diego quay. On the eastern seaboard, Avenida España hugs the coast before it joins up with the Autopista de las Américas, running east to the airport and beyond.

The Colonial City

The main site of tourist interest is the colonial city, occupying a unique niche in history as the first city in the Americas, with the first cathedral, palace, fortress, hospital, monastery, court and university to be built in the New World. It is a World Heritage Site and has undergone significant restoration works, although some sites are being left as ruins. Many of the oldest buildings can scarcely be called original, having been rebuilt after hurricanes, earthquakes, fires and pirate attacks. In fact, during the 16th and 17th centuries repair work was ongoing as the citizens struggled to cope with one disaster after another.

Fortification of the city began in 1503, although the walls were not built until 40 years later. There were 20 defensive positions, including

Bust of Bartolomé Colón, the founder of Santo Domingo

Fortaleza Ozama

six gates into the city, but not much remains today. The largest fortress, occupying the most strategic position at the mouth of the river, was the **Fortaleza Ozama** or **Fortaleza de Santo Domingo** (Mon–Sat 9am–7pm, Sun 10am–3pm; charge). The tower, **Torre de Homenaje**, was started in 1503 and from the top you can see there are two city walls, the outer one having been built by Trujillo in 1936. This is a wonderful spot from which to view the city, the river and the coastline. The **Carlos III** gate was not built until 1787 and was the third gate to be built at the fortress. The **Arsenal Polvorín de Santa Bárbara** also dates from the 18th century.

Calle Las Damas

Running north from the fortress, parallel with the river, past many of the oldest buildings, is **Calle Las Damas**. This is the oldest paved street in the town and was so named because Doña María Toledo, wife of Columbus' son Diego Colón and niece of the king of Spain, brought 30 ladies of the court with her to the colony for company and they used to walk along here. Diego was the first viceroy of the New World and the fourth governor of Santo Domingo, and he was responsible for much of the construction of the city. He and the ladies lived first in the fortress, then moved to the **Casa del Cordón**, the first stone building in the Americas, and finally to the far end of Calle Las Damas to the **Alcázar de Colón** (Mon–Sat 9am–5pm, Sun 9am–4.30pm; charge), the first palace. Diego had it built by Indian slave labour in

1510–14 without any nails and it was the seat of the Spanish Crown. Four generations of the Colón family lived here until 1577. In 1586 it was sacked by Francis Drake and only restored in 1957.

Next to the fortress is **Casa de Bastidas**, the house of Rodrigo de Bastidas, a former governor who went on to found Santa Marta in Colombia. Built of brick and stone around a shady courtyard garden, it has been converted to a **Museo Infantil** (Tue–Fri and Sun 8am–5pm, Sat 9am–6pm; charge).

Also on Calle Las Damas are the **Casa de los Dávila** and **Casa de Ovando**, two grand 16th-century houses which are now jointly restored to form a luxury hotel overlooking the river. On the other side of the road is the **Casa de Hernán Cortés**, now used as the French Embassy, which was supposedly the home of the conquistador before he went off to conquer Cuba and Mexico.

The Panteón Nacional

The **Panteón Nacional** (Tue–Sun 9am–4.30pm) was formerly a Jesuit church dating back to the 18th century, but was restored and converted into the National Pantheon by Trujillo in 1950. It contains the tombs of many of the country's heroes and dictators, but not that of Trujillo. His proposed tomb is here, but after

Strolling along Calle el Conde

his assassination he was not considered worthy to rest with patriots and is buried in Paris. The building is in the shape of a cross and in the middle hangs an ornate bronze lamp donated by General Franco of Spain.

One of the most important colonial buildings on this street is the **Museo de las Casas Reales** (daily 9am–5pm; charge), which was built at the beginning of the 16th century to house the Audiencia Real (Royal Tribunal) and the Capitanías Generales (Captaincy General). This former seat of power and justice has been extensively restored and is now used as a museum of Spanish colonial art and artefacts, along with some military pieces and furniture.

Opposite the Alcázar de Colón is an area known as **Las Atarazanas**, which was formerly the colonial dockyards. Warehouses and workshops have been converted into restaurants and bars spilling over into the **Plaza España** and it is a pleasant place to visit both day and night. There is also a museum, **Las Reales Atarazanas**, which contains items salvaged from sunken ships (daily 9am–5pm; charge).

Calle el Conde

The old city is bisected by a busy pedestrian shopping street, **Calle el Conde**, which runs from the river by the Casa de Bastidas west to the **Puerta del Conde** at the edge of the colonial zone. It passes the **Parque Colón**, the hub of social life, where you can find licensed guides to give you a tour of the city (charge negotiable). In the square there is a **statue**

of Christopher Columbus with a Taíno woman at his feet, while on the south side is the **Catedral Metropolitana Santa María de la Encarnación, Primada de América** (Mon–Sat 9am–4.30pm), the first to be built in the Americas. Construction of the church started in 1523 but it was not finished until around 1541. It became a cathedral in 1546. There is little of the original construction left, as so many architects have had a go at extending and improving it. Sir Francis Drake ransacked it in 1586, destroyed graves and records and used it as his headquarters. It also suffered hurricane and earthquake damage over the years.

Dem Bones, Dem Bones

The mystery of Columbus' bones rumbles on and his supposed remains were dug up in 2002 for the tenth time. The explorer died in Valladolid in Spain but his body was taken to Santo Domingo, where he and his son, Diego Colón, were buried in the cathedral in 1537. In 1795, when Santo Domingo was taken over by France, the bones were taken to Havana, but when the Spanish were thrown out of Cuba in 1898 they were returned to Seville. However, matters were complicated by the discovery in 1886 of an urn in the cathedral in Santo Domingo which contained bones and the inscription 'The Illustrious Don Cristóbal Colón'. Dominicans assumed these bones to be those of the man himself and in 1992 he was moved from his tomb in the cathedral to the commemorative lighthouse, the Faro a Colón. Now scientists from the University of Granada, Spain, have examined the bones of father and son, checking them against those of an illegitimate son, Hernando, , and Cristóbal's brother, Diego. They have proved that the bones in the cathedral in Seville match the mitochondrial DNA of Columbus' brother, Diego, and are therefore Cristóbal's, but this does not mean that the bones in Santo Domingo are not his as well. It is possible that the bones were divided. Further research is attempting to establish the nationality of the family.

There are 14 chapels, all with different style ceilings and dedications. Behind the altar is a monument where the supposed remains of Christopher Columbus once lay in a tomb donated by Spain in 1892.

Two historical sites have been left in ruins rather than restored. The **Monasterio de San Francisco** was the first monastery to be constructed in the New World. Started in the first half of the 16th century, it was added to in the second half but sacked by Drake. Earthquakes in 1673 and 1751 severely damaged the structure, but it was repaired. At the end of the 19th century it was used as an asylum for the insane, but hurricanes closed it down in the 1930s. The ruins have been made stable enough for the site to be used as an atmospheric venue for various cultural events, but there are no plans to rebuild.

Monasterio de San Francisco, detail

The **Hospital-Iglesia de San Nicolás de Bari** is also in ruins. Built in 1509–52 in the shape of a cross, the Gothic vaulted church had three aisles for worship while two-storey wings were hospital wards. Like all the other buildings of its age, it suffered pirate attacks, hurricanes and earthquakes, but by the beginning of the 20th century it had become dangerous and parts of the structure were demolished.

Gazcue

West of the colonial zone outside the city walls is Gazcue, also known as the new town. In the early 20th century this was the desirable place to live, with elegant villas standing in their own gardens and plenty of space, in contrast with the cluttered narrow streets of the old city.

Standing guard at the Parque Independencia

Just outside the **Puerta del Conde** two smart soldiers wearing white uniforms stand guard at the **Parque Independencia**. In the park is the **Altar de la Patria** (Altar of the Fatherland), containing the tombs of the three men who were instrumental in achieving the nation's independence. Duarte, Sánchez and Mella were first interred under stone at the entrance gate, but in 1976, on the anniversary of Duarte's death, their remains were moved to the new mausoleum containing a generous quantity of Carrara marble. Three larger than life statues overlook a well with the tomb and an eternal flame. The park is shut at 6pm to keep out prostitutes and other undesirables.

The coral pink **Palacio Presidencial** (Presidential Palace) occupies a large block south of Avenida Pedro Henríquez Ureña and west of Avenida 30 de Marzo. It was built in 1944–47 by Trujillo as a showpiece with a neoclassical central portico and cupola and is still in use by the president today. It is not regularly open to the public, but tours of the three lavish salons can be arranged in advance (tel: 809 695 8000). In

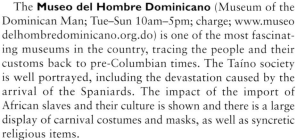

Taíno legacy

Taíno words that are still in use worldwide today include: canoe, hammock, barbecue, maize, tobacco, iguana, manatee, hurricane, savannah, and papaya.

the area around it there are several 20th-century government office buildings, the Senate and the Congress.

Plaza de la Cultura

The modern **Plaza de la Cultura** was built by President Balaguer to house the country's cultural treasures. On Avenida Máximo Gómez is the white marble **Teatro Nacional** (National Theatre), which stages ballet, drama and opera by foreign as well as national companies. Behind it is a collection of museums and the National Library.

The **Museo del Hombre Dominicano** (Museum of the Dominican Man; Tue–Sun 10am–5pm; charge; www.museo delhombredominicano.org.do) is one of the most fascinating museums in the country, tracing the people and their customs back to pre-Columbian times. The Taíno society is well portrayed, including the devastation caused by the arrival of the Spaniards. The impact of the import of African slaves and their culture is shown and there is a large display of carnival costumes and masks, as well as syncretic religious items.

The **Museo Nacional de Historia y Geografía** (Museum of History and Geography; Tue–Sun 9am–4.30pm; charge) is better, but concentrates on the 19th and 20th centuries. It is very interesting on the Haitian invasions, the US occupation and the cult of Trujillo. The **Museo de Arte Moderno** (Modern Art Museum; Tue–Sun 10am–6pm; charge) has an excellent collection of 20th-century Dominican art, with all the leading painters represented, including Jaime Colson, Candido Bidó and José Vela Zanetti, who painted murals for Trujillo among other works. Common themes run through much of the work exhibited, such as the Amerindian heritage, poverty and peasant life, and mythology.

Faro a Colón

East of the river is the grandiose Columbus Lighthouse (daily 9am–5pm; charge), erected by Balaguer to commemorate the 500th anniversary of the landing of Christopher Columbus in 1992. Built to a British design after an international competition, it is in the shape of a crucifix, with a mausoleum at the centre containing the supposed bones of the explorer *(see page 29)*. Of all his huge spending projects this was Balaguer's most controversial and extravagant. A large area of slum dwellings was cleared to make way for the lighthouse, the cost of which has been estimated at around US$40 million. The Lighthouse laser beams light up into the night sky to make the shape of a cross on the clouds. At a time when blackouts were frequent, this use of electricity was seen as wasteful. The public criticism developed into angry demonstrations. After several people were killed, international attention was attracted to the controversy. The Pope decided not to inaugurate the building after all and the king and queen of Spain declined to attend the ceremonies. In the event, not even Balaguer attended. His sister died just hours after inspecting the completed building and he remained at home in mourning while the public speculated on a possible curse, or *fukú*, put on the building by Columbus. There is still a shortage of electricity and the laser is rarely turned on, even today.

The Faro a Colón

Tres Ojos

East of the Lighthouse in the **Parque Mirador del Este**, are the *cenotes*, or limestone sinkholes known as **Tres Ojos** (Three Eyes; daily 9am–5pm; charge). These large pools in caves have been popular bathing holes since pre-Columbian times and there are legends about Taíno princesses bathing here with their ladies. Nowadays swimming is prohibited, but there are walkways for you to inspect the sulphurous and rather smelly ponds and a little pontoon ferry across one pool to another. This is quite a tourist trap and vendors outside sell handicrafts made from stalagmites and stalactites, an ecological disaster.

Jardín Botánico Nacional

The **Jardín Botánico Nacional** (National Botanic Garden) is situated to the north of the city on Avenida de los Próceres (daily 9am–5pm; charge; www.jbn-sdq.org). Established in 1976, it is dedicated to the memory of a Dominican botanist, Dr Rafael M. Moscoso, who founded the Botanical Institute at the University of Santo Domingo. Plants endemic to the island are grown here, but there are also many specimens from elsewhere. As well, there is an area of untouched forest. Several trackless trains are available to take visitors around the gardens, and a guide explains what you are seeing during your 30-minute tour. You can get off to walk around the Japanese Garden, with its pretty, manicured lawns, ponds and bridges.

Ginger lily, Botanic Garden

Laid-back Isla Saona, off the southeastern tip of the island

THE SOUTHEAST

The eastern toe of the island is edged with superb beaches and consequently this area has been quite heavily developed for tourism. The biggest hotels are all-inclusives, but given that they are remote there is not much alternative. The towns in the east are of little interest to travellers and other than the attractions of sun, sea and sand there is not much to do close by. Excursions usually involve a lot of driving.

Boca Chica

This is the closest beach resort to Santo Domingo and is very busy at weekends with families from the capital. There are a couple of large hotels in the town, but most are further east along the coast at **Juan Dolio**. Most of the hotels and guest-houses in Boca Chica are small but basic and not always safe. The town has a night time reputation for prostitution and

Merengue in Boca Chica: a band member plays the *güira*

hassling but the authorities are trying hard to clean it up. If you need assistance, the tourist office and Politur are upstairs in a little mall on Calle Duarte, the main street, at the east end.

The beach is lovely and worth visiting. Offshore there is a little island, **La Matica**, and a reef, which protect it from the waves and currents. The wide expanse of pale sand fades into the calm-as-a-swimming pool turquoise sea, perfect for children as they have to go very far out before they are out of their depth. At weekends there are dozens of stalls selling local food, rum and beer. You can choose from fried fish, sausage, sweet potato, yuca, *tostones (see page 96)*, plátano and *yaniqueque*. If you don't want the noise and crowds typical of a beach where Dominicans play, try going during the week, when it is much quieter.

Cuevas de las Maravillas

The 'Wondrous Caves' are just off the main road from San Pedro de Macorís to La Romana and if they are open are well worth a visit. A one-hour tour is offered by a knowledgeable guide through the vast cave system, where you can see stalagmites and stalactites. The caves were used by the Taíno Indians and the guide will point out their drawings as you proceed along the well-lit walkways. Maintenance works often force temporary closure, but there is a museum, shop and café (Tue–Sun 10am–6pm; charge; tel: 809 696 1797).

Casa de Campo

The exclusive resort of Casa de Campo lies just outside the sugar town of La Romana and was built on 3,000 hectares (7,500 acres) of land formerly under sugar cane. There is a small hotel, but it is primarily a luxury villa development with restaurants, bars, shops, a small beach, a marina and watersports. Its guests have a choice of three world class championship golf courses, a state-of-the-art tennis centre, horses for polo, showjumping, dressage or trekking, clay pigeon shooting and any number of other sports. An international airport is just five minutes' drive away, so there is no need for guests to venture out into the real world of the Dominican Republic.

Altos de Chavón

At the edge of Casa de Campo is **Altos de Chavón**, a folly of the highest order. An artificial, mock Italian artists' village,

Altos de Chavón

Boats at Bayahibe

it was designed by an Italian film maker and sits on the western edge of the gorge of the River Chavón. The hilltop setting is spectacular and is frequently used for wedding photo shoots outside the church of **St Stanislaus**, which was built in 1979 and consecrated by Pope John Paul II. Surprisingly, it contains the ashes of Poland's patron saint and there is a statue of him from Kraków. The chapel doors are kept open but you are barred from entering by a metal grill.

An enormous amphitheatre seating 5,500 is a feature of the village. Frank Sinatra gave the first concert here, but other international stars such as Julio Iglesias and Gloria Estefan have followed him, as well as numerous Dominicans.

The **Museo Arqueológico Regional** (daily 9am–5pm; free; www.altosdechavon.com/fs_museum.htm) is the best archaeological museum in the country and has an excellent collection of Amerindian artefacts from this region. The beliefs of the Taínos are well explained with examples of their idols representing deities, many of them animals. The rest of the village comprises restaurants, shops and the art school, catering for students from all over the world.

Bayahibe

The unpretentious fishing village of **Bayahibe** now has a split personality. While you can still find fishing boats pulled up on the beach in the little bay, outside the village along the coast there are several large resorts. In the village there are a couple of small hotels and dozens of cheap *cabañas* for rent. Despite the influx of tourism it remains a low key, laid back place with several decent restaurants, bars and cafés around the bay.

The reason that so many people come to this tiny place is the **Parque Nacional del Este** (National Park of the East), which covers all the peninsula to the east and south of Bayahibe and offshore, including **Isla Saona**, **Isla Catalina** and **Catalinita**. Saona Island is very popular as an excursion, with boats taking around 1,000 visitors a day to sit on the beach, have a picnic lunch and return via a sand bank in the sea where the water is shallow and as clear as a swimming pool. Catalina and Catalinita islands are also popular for day trips with snorkelling and scuba diving. The underwater world is spectacular, with the reef occupied by colourful fish of all shapes and sizes. Dolphins often follow the dive boats, while sharks and rays live off Catalinita. This is where the Atlantic Ocean meets the Caribbean Sea; there are millions of shells on a small, sandy beach, crayfish and shrimp in the shallow water and then coral, giant sponges, sea fans and lots of fish in the deeper water, all great for snorkelling.

A diver's dream

On land, this remote part of the island is covered with a mixture of subtropical humid forest and inhospitable dry forest with a large number of endemic trees and birds. Although it is uninhabited now, there is plenty of evidence that the Taínos lived here. Caves in the park contain pictographs (drawings) and petrographs (carvings) and many of the relics now housed in museums were discovered here. Archaeologists have found the remains of a large settlement with three plazas and a ball court which is believed to have been the site of a Spanish massacre of rebellious Indians. Only a few caves are accessible; a fair amount of effort is required, take insect repellent.

Higüey

Inland from Bayahibe across cattle ranches and sugar cane plantations, **Higüey** lies at the foothills of the Cordillera Oriental. It was important as the seat of the Higüey *cacigazco* (chiefdom) in pre-Columbian times and is still important today as the provincial capital. It is not a beautiful city, being mostly a 20th-century creation with an over-reliance on concrete, but it has one site of interest. The **Basílica de Nuestra Señora de la Altagracia** was begun by Trujillo in 1954 but not completed until 1972. It is the most impressive piece of modern architecture in the country, designed by French architects, and the huge arched roof of the nave can be seen for miles around. It stands grandly in a large park in the centre of town which,

Higüey's modern basilica

every year on 21 January is packed with pilgrims and worshippers celebrating Our Lady of Altagracia, the patroness of the Republic. The statue of the Virgin and a silver crown in a glass case are paraded through the streets accompanied by a brass band the morning after a long night of vigil and partying. The Virgin is supposed to have appeared in an orange tree to a sick girl, and oranges are a feature of the fiesta. Piles of fruit are sold in the streets along with statues carved from orange wood. Inside the Basilica orange wood is used extensively and the orange tree is a recurring theme.

Bávaro and Punta Cana

The extreme eastern tip of the island is blessed with glorious beaches, miles and miles of pale golden sand shaded by thousands of coconut palms. It was here, therefore, that the governments of the 1980s and 1990s decided to promote tourism and allow the building of massive resorts along the coast. The first hotel, *Club Med*, opened in 1981, followed by the *Punta Cana Beach Resort* in 1988. An international airport was built at Punta Cana and construction began in a big way, with golf courses, marinas and other tourist attractions accompanying the hotels. Guests are taken on trips into the countryside or to Bayahibe and Isla Saona for diving and a change of scenery on the beach, but it is a long way to Santo Domingo or the rest of the island, requiring a lot of driving or the expense of internal flights. Few people leave their hotels other than on organised excursions, but in between the all-inclusives there are the remains of fishing villages, a few

> **Beware coconuts!**
>
> Worldwide, some 10–12 people die annually from shark attacks, but around 150 are killed by falling coconuts. Hotel keepers usually prune the coconuts from the palm trees on their property, but watch where you sit, even small, immature coconuts fall sometimes and can do you serious damage.

Unspoilt beach at Miches

shacks struggling to hang on. There is little housing in the area so far, with workers brought in from Higüey and other towns in the region, but there are plans to build a whole town here, and roads are being laid out.

If you do hire a car, a pleasant day's drive is from Otra Banda, just east of Higüey, north up to the coast to the **Reserva Cientifica Lagunas Redonda y Limón**, a unique bird sanctuary with two shallow lagoons. You can follow the coast road through **Miches**, where there is a pleasant hotel with a great view for miles and some deserted, unspoilt beaches, to **Sabana de la Mar**. Boat trips into Parque Nacional Los Haitises *(see page 73)* leave from here and port construction is scheduled to enable improved ferry service to Samaná, across the bay. You can return through Hato Mayor and El Seibo, two agricultural towns in the mountains of the Cordillera Oriental, to Higüey and the east coast. Major road building is planned to link all the resorts around the coast to Miches and Sabana de la Mar.

THE SOUTHWEST

A good road, the Carretera Sánchez, leads west along the coast from Santo Domingo through progressively drier countryside. After Azua it heads northwest through the Valle de San Juan to the Haitian border at Elias Piña. Most traffic, however, follows the coastal road to Barahona, from where there is another road to the Haitian border at Jimaní. This is a hot, dry area with several mountain ranges and cultivated valleys. The closer you get to Haiti, the fewer trees there are, but National Parks have been established to protect large areas of forest and coastline.

San Cristóbal

The dictator, Trujillo, was born in San Cristóbal and maintained a home here throughout his life. He even changed its name to Meritorious City but it reverted back to its original name after his assassination. It was when he was travelling to the town to visit a mistress that he was gunned down on the outskirts of the capital in 1961. Both of his houses can be visited if you can attract the attention of the guardians: the **Casa de Caoba** (Mahogany House) was once lined with mahogany but is now stripped bare. Much of the furniture has been stored in his other property, **El Castillo del Cerro** (the Castle on the Hill). This large, hideous, block-built building on the hill, with a view as far as Santo Domingo, is in slightly better condition and under the control of the military.

Relaxing in Barahona

Sugar cane harvest near Baní

For a tip a soldier will show you around the gutted 1945 mansion, where the remaining opulent decoration gives an idea of his family's lifestyle. The ceilings are still mostly intact, with moulding in pink and chocolate or pistachio and cream, looking for all the world like frosting on a cake. There is still some mosaic tiling in the bathrooms, together with several green bath tubs. In one salon there is a Vela Zanetti mural which Trujillo commissioned to show typical Dominicans in party mode, but while they are dancing, not one face appears cheerful and no one is enjoying it.

Baní

The small town of **Baní** is surrounded by sugar cane fields, and sugar is still the main industry. In the cane cutting season in the first half of the year you will see gangs of workers labouring in the fields and ox-drawn carts laden with canes on their way to the mill. There is also some salt production at **Las Salinas**, about 30km (18 miles) from Baní, where **Punta Salinas** is a finger of land jutting out on the south side of the **Bahía las Calderas**. There are huge sand dunes at Las Calderas which have now been made a National Monument, and at Las Salinas there is good windsurfing and fishing.

Baní itself is famous for being the birthplace of Máximo Gómez, who went to Cuba to fight in the independence wars there in the 19th century. His house is now a museum, open to the public (daily 8am–noon; free) with photographs and historical documents about his life.

Barahona

An international airport has been built at **Barahona** to promote the development of tourism in the area, but so far little has happened and the region remains quiet. The town itself is nothing special, and has been in decline since the closing of the sugar mill. The Haitian ruler, Toussaint L'Ouverture, founded the town in 1802, when he controlled the whole island, and developed a thriving port for the export of mahogany and other hard woods. Creaking, rusting ships can still be seen in the port, plying their trade along the coast. There are a few cheap hotels in town, but there are nicer places to stay at **Baoruco**, 16km (10 miles) south down the coast where the sea is less polluted.

Just before you reach Baoruco, about 14km (9 miles) from Barahona, there is a village called **Las Filipinas**. At the southern end of the village, if you turn right along a dirt track you

Bahoruco Beach Resort, down the coast from Barahona

will eventually come to the **larimar mines**. Four-wheel-drive is essential for this potholed but beautiful drive up into the mountains through forest filled with wild flowers and butterflies and occasional glimpses of a tremendous view down to the sea. Don't go if it has been raining, as not only will the track be impassable but the mines will be flooded and there is unlikely to be anyone there. At the very end of the track you come to the mine worked by the Cooperativa Bahoruco, a co-operative of 450 miners. The side of the mountain, stripped bare by the works, is pockmarked with holes. Tiny tunnels supported by rickety timber struts disappear into the dark, where the men work in the constant wet to hack out lumps of stone in the hope of finding larimar. You will be expected to buy rough cut stones of all shapes and sizes, which are sold by weight, but the men are very friendly and informative and are happy to show you around. At weekends artisans from Santo

Iguanas are a common sight

Domingo make the journey to buy stones for the jewellery market.

The road south of Barahona runs along the coast, with lovely scenery of mountains and rivers tumbling into the sea. There are several beaches, although most are pebbles rather than sand, and you will find domestic animals and their droppings. In places where there are

Bird of Paradise flower

rivers, there are freshwater bathing holes, which are usually safer for swimming than the sea as the waves can be large.

Parque Nacional Jaragua

At the southern end of the bulge of the Sierra de Baoruco, is the **Parque Nacional Jaragua** (Jaragua National Park; daily 8.30am–4.30pm; charge; www.grupojaragua.org.do/pnj.html). This is the largest of all the protected areas in the country, comprised mainly of subtropical dry forest, thorn scrub and cactus, although there are mangroves, mahogany and frangipani. It is also a marine sanctuary and includes the uninhabited islands of **Isla Beata** and **Isla Alto Velo**, as well as the **Laguna Oviedo**, where there are huge numbers of flamingos, herons, spoonbill and frigate birds. Iguanas are common and you can find both the Ricord and rhinoceros types. Boat trips are available on the lake with a Spanish-speaking guide.

There are some lovely beaches in the National Park, **Bahía de las Aguilas** being particularly beautiful, and there is constant pressure to build hotels within the park, partly to provide jobs for the people of **Pedernales** on the Haitian border, but so far no development has taken place.

Lake Enriquillo is the lowest point of the Caribbean islands

Lago Enriquillo

Sandwiched between the Sierra de Neiba to the north and the 800 sq km (300 sq mile) **Parque Nacional Sierra de Baoruco** to the south is a large flat-bottomed valley, the Valle de Neiba. **Lago Enriquillo** (Lake Enriquillo; charge) covers 200 sq km (75 sq miles) of this valley and it is unusual in that it lies 44m (144ft) below sea level. Its water is therefore three times more salty than the sea and an ideal habitat for flamingos, iguanas and crocodiles. Geologists think that the lake was once connected to the bay of Port-au-Prince (the capital of Haiti to the west) but that it was cut off by tectonic movements. Coral and ancient sea shells have been found on the beaches and in the hills. Lago Enriquillo is on the Ramsar list of Wetlands of International Importance and the core of the Enriquillo–Bahoruco–Jaragua Biosphere Reserve.

In the middle of the lake is **Isla Cabritos**, also a National Park, which is the best place to see the 500 American crocodiles that live on the lake. Boat trips go out when there are enough people. It is extremely hot and dry, only cactus grows here; take water, sun screen and a hat. There are iguanas everywhere and a few can be aggressive in asking for food.

Just east of the Park entrance on the north side of the lake is **Las Caritas**. Stop at the side of the road and scramble up the rocks to an arch, or small cave, on the hillside, where there are Taíno pictographs. Faces *(caritas)* have been etched in the coral rock. It is pleasant to sit in the shade of the arch and admire the view over the lake to the mountains in the distance.

To the west of the lake is one of the busiest border crossings, at **Jimaní**. In May 2004, the town was at the centre of one of the worst natural disasters ever to hit the Dominican Republic. Here alone, hundreds of people were killed in flash floods and mudslides caused by torrential rains that wrought destruction on both sides of the border.

Reserva Científica Laguna Rincón

The road from Barahona to Lake Enriquillo and Jimaní passes the hamlet of **Cabral**, and just beyond it lies **Laguna Rincón**, also known as Laguna Cabral, a 47 sq km (18 sq mile) freshwater lake, the largest in the country and a habitat for turtles, flamingos, herons and other water birds. Boat trips are available from the park office at Cabral where you pay your admission fee.

Further along, at the junction of the **Neiba** road, is the memorial to the Taíno chieftain Enriquillo, who fought long and hard, but ultimately in vain, against the Spanish *(see page 13)*.

Seeing is believing

A turning at Cabral marked 'Polo' will take you to one of the world's strangest optical illusions. At a place called Polo Magnético, the road appears to slope upwards and if you place a ball on the road it seems to run uphill, as does your car if you put it in neutral.

The Jimenoa Falls in the Dominican Alps, near Jarabacoa

THE INTERIOR

The Autopista Duarte, a four-lane toll road, runs northwest out of Santo Domingo along the agricultural Cibao Valley to the country's second city, Santiago de los Caballeros. The range of mountains on your left is the Cordillera Central, with the highest mountains and some of the most stunning scenery on the island. As you climb up into the mountains the air becomes noticeably cooler and more pleasant. The perfume of pine trees freshens the air, rivers rush over boulders and through gorges and wild flowers tumble down banks like the waterfalls below. There is so much to do if you are fit and active, with opportunities for hiking, horse riding, river rafting, canyoning, tubing, quad bikes, mountain bikes and other sports.

Constanza

Constanza is a small town in the middle of a large, circular valley in the mountains. The soil is amazingly fertile and productive and this is the vegetable garden for the country. Huge cabbages, potatoes, garlic, onions, cauliflowers, strawberries and other temperate zone crops are harvested here, while some enormous greenhouses produce tomatoes and flowers for export. Although there are records of a few people living here in the 19th century, there were still less than 100 huts in 1930. It was Trujillo who promoted immigration in the 1950s, encouraging settlers from Spain, Japan and Eastern Europe for their farming knowledge, while Lebanese brought their trading skills (the name Tactuk is still seen above stores in town). The population now amounts to around 80,000, of whom 95 percent are involved in farming. Tourism is low key but Constanza is popular with locals for weekend breaks and Dominicans on holiday here outnumber foreigners.

One local attraction is the **Aguas Blancas** waterfall, at 87m (285ft) the highest in the Caribbean. It is about 15km (9 miles) from Constanza on the road to San José de Ocoa. From the signposted turning you need four-wheel-drive (or walk) for the last 1.5km (1 mile), which is very rough. You can see the waterfall from the road, but there is a path and a metal staircase to get to the pool at the foot of the fall. You can swim there if you can stand the freezing cold water. Brave

'Fly Me to Constanza...'

Although Constanza owed its existence to Trujillo, who built roads, civic buildings, a school, church, hospital, hotel, airstrip and other public works to encourage immigration, the town also played a part in his downfall. On 14 June 1959, a plane carrying anti-Trujillo guerrillas landed at the airport. Led by a Cuban commander fresh from the successful Cuban Revolution, the men scattered into the mountains. Their quest to topple another Caribbean dictator failed, however, and they were hunted down and killed or 'disappeared'. Local collaborators were imprisoned, tortured and murdered, but the seeds of rebellion were sown. The 14th June Movement (Movimiento 14 de Junio) became the focus for Dominican resistance and two years later Trujillo was shot.

souls jump in from the cliff overlooking the pool. If it has rained, the water is usually brown, but at other times it is totally clear and the ultimate in 'refreshing'.

Further along the Ocoa road is the **Parque Nacional Valle Nuevo**, where the mountain scenery is reminiscent of the Alps with pine forests and farmsteads perched on ledges. It is at an altitude of around 2,250m (7,500ft), with several small valleys, one of which is appropriately named La Nevera (the fridge), where temperatures of −6°C (21°F) have been recorded. There are many endemic plant species here and the area is great for bird watching. On the way, you pass the geographical centre of the island, where Trujillo built a pyramid in 1956.

Heading for the river

Jarabacoa

Continuing north on the Autopista Duarte, you will arrive at the town of **La Vega**. From here it's well worth making a detour west to **Jarabacoa**, which lies in an area known as the **Dominican Alps**, the centre of adventure tourism offering excellent hiking, riding, biking and river sports. People come here before climbing Pico Duarte or other hikes into the National Parks. Pine forests cling to the hillsides around the town and there are several rivers flowing into one another. The River Baiguate flows into the

Jimenoa, which then joins up with the River Yaque del Norte, heading northwest to empty into the sea at Monte Cristi. On these and their tributaries you can go river rafting, tubing, canyoning and kayaking.

Within reach of the town are two impressive waterfalls. The **Baiguate Falls** are about 4km (2½ miles) away but there are tours by horse or vehicle if you don't want

Sorting beans at the Café La Joya coffee factory

to walk. There is a pleasant pool at the foot of the falls, with a sandy beach and boulders to sit on. Larger and with considerably more water are the **Jimenoa Falls**, about 10km (6 miles) away, where a hydroelectricity plant provides power for the town, repaired after Hurricane George washed away the previous plant and bridge in 1998. A series of very rickety suspension bridges leads to the falls, but have a habit of swaying alarmingly if there are too many people on them (charge). The water cascades 20m (65ft) and you can take a refreshing shower underneath.

The town itself is modern and nothing special architecturally, but it is friendly and busy. It is a popular weekend retreat, with a comfortable climate, warm days and cool nights. Farming is excellent, with lots of fruit and vegetables such as strawberries and watercress, as well as flowers for export. You can visit the local coffee factory, **Café La Joya**, where staff will explain the whole production process from cultivation to coffee cup. There is a small gift shop where local arts and crafts are sold alongside everything coffee – even coffee candles with coffee beans in them.

Pico Duarte

Although it is agreed that **Pico Duarte** is the highest mountain in the Caribbean, the recorded height varies. In the time of the dictator Trujillo, when it was renamed Pico Trujillo, it was claimed to be 3,187m (10,456ft), which is still on most maps today, but it is believed that a more accurate reading is 3,087m (10,128ft), making it only slightly higher than its neighbour, La Pelona, at 3,082m (10,111ft). Hiking up the mountain is one of the most rewarding activities on the island. On your way up to the top, where there is a bust of Duarte, you pass through several different ecosystems and the forest changes from rainforest to pine forest as you get higher. There are lots of birds, flowers and butterflies, and the views are tremendous.

Pico Duarte, the highest mountain in the Caribbean

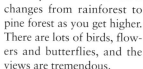

The mountain is on the border of the **Parque Nacional Armando Bermúdez** and the **Parque Nacional José del Carmen Ramírez**, and as with all national parks in the DR, you have to pay a fee and you may not enter without a guide. You can hire a guide privately and he will arrange for mules to carry all the gear, or you can book in with an agency such as Rancho Baiguate in Jarabacoa, or Iguana Mama in Cabarete, who offer hikes of two days or more. They provide the guides, transport, food, tents and other equipment. The most popular route to the top starts from La Ciénaga, near Jarabacoa. The National Parks office is 4km (2½ miles) from here and the trail is a total of 46km (29 miles). After about six hours' walk there is a hut at La Compartición, where people spend the night. The peak is about two hours' climb from here, so you can start early next

Hiking Pico Duarte

The climb to the top of Pico Duarte is no stroll. It is essential that you hire reliable guides and that you are prepared for an arduous trek. Warm clothing is a must, as temperatures can fall below freezing at night. The best months are between November and March when there is less chance of heavy rain.

morning to get to the top and all the way down again the same day. There are other, more demanding trails, some starting from other entrances to the Park. The 90km (56-mile) trail from Mata Grande near San José de las Matas is one.

Santo Cerro

A further excursion can be made from La Vega to the holy mountain of **Santo Cerro**, a centre of pilgrimage off the road from La Vega to Moca. The church of early-colonial design but dating from 1886 is perched on top of the hill up a steep road. Directly in front of it is a cross, and a tree next to it bears a plaque announcing that it came from the same tree *(níspero)* that Christopher Columbus used to make the first ever crucifix here. And thereby hangs a tale: in 1495 the Taínos rose up against their Spanish overlords on the Santo Cerro under the leadership of Guarionex. Just as they were about to set fire to the cross placed here by Columbus – so the story goes – the Virgen de las Mercedes appeared, protected the Christian symbol and forced the Indians to subjugate themselves. A section of the original cross is apparently preserved inside the church.

The church at Santo Cerro

Turn left on your descent in the direction of Pueblo Viejo and Moca. A sign on the left points to the Parque Nacional Histórico La Vega Vieja, preserving the ruins of **La Vega Vieja** (open most days, always at weekends 9am–2pm or 3pm), a settlement founded by Columbus. Well worth seeing here are the **Ruinas Convento San Francisco**, the remains of the Franciscan monastery which was built in 1502. The foundation walls show the outlines of different sections of the first monastery built on American soil: the chapel, the well and the cloister. Nearby is the **Fortaleza Nuestra Señora de la Concepción** – the fortress built by Columbus after his victory over the Taínos in 1495. One tower, with arrow-slits, is quite well preserved. A museum nearby contains several everyday items, both Taíno and Spanish, that were unearthed on the site.

Salcedo

From **Moca**, a well-surfaced road (Carretera 132) leads eastwards along the edge of the Cibao Valley to **Salcedo**. The landscape is delightful, filled with banana plants, palm trees and coconut palms, and villages of brightly-painted wooden houses line the road. At the entrance to Salcedo is a square with a modern metal sculpture. Portraits on the wall enclosing the square commemorate the Tres Hermanas Mirabal. They were placed here in 1990 for the 30th anniversary of the deaths of the three Mirabal sisters, who were shot by Trujillo's thugs on 25 November 1960, six months before his dictatorship

came to an end. About 5km (3 miles) beyond Salcedo at
Conuco, in their family home built in 1954, is the **Museo de
las Hermanas Mirabal** (daily 9.30am–5pm; charge), containing photographs and belongings of the three sisters, Patria,
Minerva and Maria Teresa, who died aged 36, 33 and 25;
items include jewellery, clothing, a bloodstained handkerchief
and the cap of their chauffeur who also died in the attack. In
the beautiful gardens are the graves of the three sisters and
Manolo, Minerva's husband, moved here from the cemetery
on the 40th anniversary of their assassination. The mausoleum
has been declared an extension of the Panteón Nacional *(see
page 27)*. The story of the sisters is recounted by Julia Alvarez
in *In the Time of the Butterflies (see below)*.

Julia Alvarez' Novels

Julia Alvarez was born in the Dominican Republic at the time of the Trujillo dictatorship, but her family emigrated to the USA in 1960. Two of
her novels, *How The García Girls Lost Their Accents* and *¡Yo!* explore the
problems of loss of homeland and difficulties of assimilating a new culture as seen through the eyes of four sisters growing up in America. They
are humorous and light hearted novels while delving into issues common to all uprooted families. For anyone interested in political repression under Trujillo, *In the Time of the Butterflies* is essential reading. The
novel follows the lives of the Mirabal sisters, who were involved through
marriage and friendship with the resistance movement and were murdered by the dictator's henchmen when returning over the mountains
from a visit to their husbands in prison in Puerto Plata. Alvarez' most
recent novel, *In the Name of Salomé*, is about another Dominican hero-
ine, Salomé Ureña, who overcame prejudice and political oppression in
the 19th century to become the national poet. The story is narrated by
her daughter, Camila, who leaves her home in the USA to discover her
roots and bond with the mother who died when she was only three.

The north coast is fringed with glorious beaches

THE NORTH COAST

The north coast is stunningly beautiful and also very varied. At the far west, the climate is arid and the vegetation mostly scrub and cactus, seemingly inhabited by more goats than people. However, the coastal strip in the shadow of the mountain range called the Cordillera Septentrional, is lush and green, fringed with golden sand beaches. This was one of the first areas to be developed for tourism in the 1980s and there are lots of resorts, golf courses and watersports on offer.

Santiago de los Caballeros

Separated from the coast by the Cordillera Septentrional, Santiago, the second city, is the main commercial centre in the north. It is a busy, modern city with a great deal of US influence. Broad, four-lane highways fan out from the centre, lined with shopping malls, fast food restaurants and shiny glass office blocks and banks, while huge advertising hoardings clutter the view. There is not a great deal of interest to tourists and it is more pleasant to stay on the beach and make a day trip to the city if there is something you want to do.

The old town is small, numbering a few blocks around **Parque Duarte**. The cathedral, **Catedral de Santiago Apóstol**, is here, a 19th-century neoclassical building, which contains the graves of some of the 19th-century leaders of the Republic. Other buildings from the same period include the **Centro de Recreo**, a private club noted for its Moorish-style arches, and the **Casa de Cultura de Santiago** in the Antiguo Palacio Consistorial (Mon–Sat 8am–6pm), which holds art exhibitions and cultural displays. The nearby **Fortaleza San Luís** has an imposing view over the River Yaque del Norte and the Cibao Valley, but it is still in military use and not open to the public.

The main shopping street in this part of town is **Calle del Sol**, which leads away from Parque Duarte up to the main landmark in the city. The **Monumento a los Héroes de la Restauración** is a huge tower on top of the highest hill, commissioned by Trujillo for his own glory, but now honouring those who fought for the restoration of the Republic (*see page 17*). You can climb to the top for panoramic views, passing the remains of a Vela Zanetti mural on the staircase portraying workers in their quest for freedom from tyranny. The large open space around the monument comes alive at carnival time or for other fiestas, and even at weekends it can be busy. Stalls are set up to sell, rum, beer and local food in addition to the many

Catedral de Santiago Apóstol

restaurants along the road all round the edge. Behind the monument is a **theatre** built by Balaguer in the 1980s. Despite its ugly, ostentatious appearance, it is the venue for all the best concerts and theatrical events in the north.

On the edge of town on Avenida 27 de Febrero is the **León Jiménez cigar factory**, which celebrated its centenary in 2003 by recreating the first cigar ever produced there in a limited edition. Even if you don't smoke, it is fascinating to visit this modern factory and see the hall where cigars are still made by hand. Each worker has a target of 100 cigars a day. You will be given a tour followed by a free drink and an opportunity to buy cigars. Alongside is the new **Centro Cultural Eduardo León Jiménez** (entry to exhibitions Tue–Sun 9am–7pm; charge), the leading exponent of Dominican culture on the north coast, if not in the whole country.

Egret in the mangroves at Monte Cristi

Monte Cristi

Continuing northwest from Santiago, the highway follows the River Yaque del Norte along the Valle del Cibao until it reaches the sea at **Monte Cristi**, a small coastal town which used to make its living from salt. It is in a very dry area of the country and as you approach the vegetation changes from fields of rice to scrub and cactus, with goats running all over the place. Offshore there is a cluster of cays known as the **Cayos Siete Hermanos** (Seven Brothers), and these, as well as the surrounding sea and the land either side of the town now form part of the **Parque Nacional Monte Cristi**, protecting mangroves and the ecosystem in general.

The town was once a thriving port with a railway. Some of the fine 19th-century merchants' houses are being renovated by the Pat

Clock tower in the Parque del Reloj

rimonio Cultural, including one called Doña Emilia's House, a huge wooden structure from 1895 with impressive verandas, grand entrance stairway and rich decorative detail. One interesting site is the **Parque del Reloj**, where a large clock tower has stood since it was brought from France in 1895.

If you drive north around the bay, past the salt pans and the yacht club, you are faced with a huge flat-topped mountain, known as **El Morro**, which dominates the landscape. There are steps up the side, used on 21 January for a pilgrimage for the Virgen de la Altagracia, when thousands of people make it to the top to pray. It is very windy on top and mini tornadoes are a regular feature of the weather. There is a small beach at the bottom, known as **Playa Detrás del Morro**, and another between the salt pans and the sea, called **Playa Juan de Bolaños**, but neither is any great attraction. For excellent snorkelling, diving or even fishing, you should take an excursion by boat out to the Cayos Siete Hermanos.

In case of attack

A garrison of 5,000 men were stationed at the fortress of La Citadelle. It is estimated that they and the royal family and court could withstand a siege of a year.

A Trip into Haiti

Just 24km (15 miles) from Monte Cristi is the border town of **Dajabón**. A huge market has grown up here, with kitchen utensils, food and counterfeit designer jeans jostling for space. It is a fascinating experience to visit and get a flavour of Haiti, with its mass of impoverished humanity, but take care and guard your possessions carefully, taking only the minimum with you.

Dajabón is the gateway to one of the most impressive sights on the entire island, the fortress of **La Citadelle** near Cap Haïtien. Perched atop the 900m (3,000ft) high Pic La Ferrière, it was built in 1805–20 by an ex-slave who called himself King Henri Christophe. After the assassination of Toussaint L'Ouverture, who led the slave rebellion and gained independence for Haiti, Christophe controlled the north of the island. His fortress was intended to deter any French reinvasion as well as to keep a firm hold on his 'kingdom' by commanding a view over the northern plain and controlling access from the sea to the central plateau. The enormous building is a tremendous feat of construction, covering 10,000 sq m (110,000 sq ft); 20,000 men were pressed into labour to build the walls up to 40m (130ft) high and 4m (13ft) thick.

Christophe also built himself a palace in the foothills below La Citadelle. **Sans Souci** was his administrative capital, with a hospital, school, printing press, clothing factory, distillery and other civil and military works. However, after Christophe shot himself in the heart with a silver bullet in 1820, the palace was ransacked by the people and later destroyed by an earthquake in 1840.

As a result of political upheavals, you should always take local advice before planning a trip into Haiti.

Puerto Plata

The main town on the north coast is **Puerto Plata**, with a port and an airport serving the beach resorts of the area. Columbus named the bay the silver port because of the glistening sun on the sea, but the town was founded by Nicolás de Ovando in 1502. The Spanish first used it as a stopping off place for the silver fleet on its way from Peru and Mexico to Spain, but other traders visited, buying hides and meat from buccaneers, as did pirates in their search for booty. In the 19th century it became an important outlet for produce from Santiago and the Cibao Valley, particularly tobacco. Merchants built grand houses in the town, which can still be seen today, and there was considerable German influence in trade. Sugar became more important in the 20th century when the Americans became involved, but boom turned to bust and local prosperity declined. The construction of the Playa Dorada tourist

Shady veranda in Puerto Plata

complex just outside town in the 1980s brought employment to the area, but the town itself has been slightly neglected.

The seafront drive, the **Malecón**, used to be an elegant boulevard, stretching the length of the town from the spit of land at the entrance to the harbour, but the apartment blocks are now tired and weatherbeaten. It is still used at Carnival time and for outdoor discos, but is in need of renovation. The government has, however, invested in beach improvement works and drainage so that Long Beach, which stretches to the east, is less polluted than it used to be. The harbour is guarded by the solid fortress built in 1540, the **Fortaleza de San Felipe** *(see picture on page 15)*. Once the age of pirates and invasions was over, the fortress was used as a prison, housing many political prisoners in the 19th and 20th centuries, but was renovated in the 1990s as a museum (daily 9am–5pm; charge). Alongside it on the highest point of the promontory is a 24m (80ft) iron **lighthouse**, built in 1879 and restored in 2002. A spiral staircase up the middle is supported by mustard coloured iron columns, while on the top is an octagonal iron cupola which used to house a revolving light fuelled by kerosene. Around the base are bits of fortress walls and cannon, and restoration work is ongoing.

Amber specimen

The **Museo del Ambar** (Amber Museum; Mon–Sat 9am–6pm; charge; www. ambermuseum.com) is in an elegant house built in 1918, intricately painted white and gold. Upstairs, the museum exhibits some fascinating pieces of amber found in the mountains behind Puerto Plata, the Cordillera Septentrional. Dominican amber is about 20–60 million years old, younger than some of the deposits found in Europe and therefore lighter, but showing clearly the insects, leaves and other debris trapped in the resin as it flowed down the tree. A piece with a lizard in it is 50 million years old. The latest find, which is of great scientific interest, encases a feather, believed to have belonged to a bird with a wingspan of 30cm (12ins). There is also 'blue' amber, the most valuable, which has volcanic ash trapped inside it. Downstairs there is a gift shop selling amber and larimar jewellery.

Getting around town

There are glorious **beaches** east and west of Puerto Plata, where resorts and villas have been built. To the west are Playa Costambar, Playa Cofresí and the Bahía de Maimón, while to the east is Playa Dorada with its enclave of all-inclusive hotels and golf course. At Cofresí presidential approval was granted, despite energetic opposition from conservation and animal welfare groups, for the construction in 2003 of the largest dolphinarium in the Caribbean. Dolphins caught in the wild by Cuba and sold to the investors have been trained to entertain tourists. **Ocean World Adventure Park** is now the leading tourist attraction on the north coast, with sea lions, sharks and sting rays completing the 'encounter' programme.

Puerto Plata is overlooked by the 779m (2,556ft) **Loma Isabel de Torres** (Isabel de Torres hill), on which stands a statue of Christ (Cristo Redentor) looking down on His flock. It is possible to hike up to the top, although you are recommended to go with an organised group as it is easy to get lost on the mountain and there are poisonous plants. The hike takes about 2 hours, but it's almost as much fun to go on the cable car *(teleférico)* from just outside town off the ring road (Circunvalación del Sur; Thur–Tue 8.30am–5pm; charge). At the top there are some nice gardens with a wonderful view of the surrounding brilliant green mountains and down to the

La Isabela: stones mark the probable positions of houses

sea. Make sure you don't go on a cloudy day when the top is shrouded in fog. There are gift shops and a restaurant, if you want to make a day of it.

Parque Nacional Ruinas de la Isabela

Situated on a promontory overlooking a sheltered bay about 44km (28 miles) west of Puerto Plata, **La Isabela** (daily 8am–5.45pm; charge) was the first Spanish settlement in the Americas. It was established by Columbus, who landed here on 29 May 1493, his second voyage, with 1,500 men on 17 ships. Today, practically the only remains able to be seen are the packed earth and cut

limestone foundations of the
Columbus House (the oldest
remnant of a European
structure in the Americas)
and the outlines of a large
warehouse and a church, as
well as some graves and
an uncovered skeleton from
a Christian burial. There
would have been more, but
when told to clean up the site
before a visit by Trujillo, an
enthusiastic official had the

Boat hands in Sosúa

ruins bulldozed and pushed into the sea. Archaeologists have
placed stones where they believe houses were located. There
is a small museum containing artefacts unearthed from the
site, a café, gift shop and guides.

Sosúa

Sosúa is a small town east of Puerto Plata with probably the
prettiest town beach in the country, a lovely curved bay with
pale golden sand and trees coming down almost to the water's
edge for shade. Under the trees is a row of stalls selling food,
drinks, hair braiding and handicrafts. At one end of the bay
luxury hotels have been built on the cliffs, while at the other
end there are a few restaurants overlooking the beach in an
area of housing known as Los Charamicos. The hotels, bars,
restaurants and most shops are in a district called El Batey,
which was settled by German Jewish refugees in 1941. Most
of the original immigrants have moved away, but their syna-
gogue is still open for services. Although tourism in Sosúa is
past its heyday, the town having lost out in the battle with all-
inclusive beach resorts, it is still a lively, cheerful place. There
are plenty of activities including a variety of watersports.

Cabarete is good for novices as well as experts

Cabarete

Still heading east along the coast, **Cabarete** is the next small town on a large, sweeping curve of sand fed by breezes which are absolutely perfect for wind- and kite-surfing. Once just a little fishing village, its sailing advantages were discovered by French Canadians and now Cabarete is world famous for windsurfing, with international competitions held here annually. Kite-surfing is usually confined to the west part of the bay at El Encuentro beach, while windsurfing takes place all along the bay. The trade winds are best in the afternoons when the sea becomes a mass of colour as the sails and kites flit about like birds in the air or butterflies on the water.

Cabarete is a mecca for active and sporty visitors, with lots of energetic things to do, such as surfing, diving, mountain biking and horse riding. A string of bars and restaurants right on the beach provide more entertainment after dark, with lots of good food, music and dancing. However, if you want to take it more gently, the beach is superb for lounging or strolling. And if you're there in mid-February, don't miss the annual sandcastle competion, held on the Castillos de Arena weekend.

Inland, behind the town there is a lagoon and some caves, part of the **Parque Nacional El Choco** (charge). A guide will explain the Taíno heritage and give you a tour on a nature trail through the forest.

Río San Juan

The main attraction here is the **Laguna Gri Grí**, where you can take boat trips from the lake in the town through the mangroves. The captains usually include local beaches and snorkelling as part of the package. Diving here is excellent as there are plenty of reefs and lots of colourful fish, and dive boats come from all along the north coast for day trips.

The curve of the coastline which bulges out from Río San Juan has several wonderful beaches, some of which are being developed for tourism. **Playa Caletón** is great for snorkelling with crystal clear water and a large rock in the middle. At weekends it is popular with Dominicans and vendors sell fried fish on the beach.

Playa Grande is, as the name suggests, one of the biggest white sand beaches in the country and can also be one of the best places to come for surfing when there is a swell in winter. Boogie boards are for hire on the beach, but if you want something more high-tech hire it in Cabarete. Don't be put off by the presence of all-inclusive hotels as there is public access to the beach.

Playa La Preciosa is less busy but also good for surfing and very photogenic. It is located in the **Parque Nacional Cabo Frances Viejo**, a small national park on the headland from where you

Kids at Playa Grande

Coconut palms line the coast

can sometimes see humpback whales between January and March. Around the headland at **Playa Diamante** the water is very shallow and you can wade out for around 75m (80yds) before you are out of your depth. It faces east, so the morning is the best time to visit for full sun. The village of **La Entrada** has a long, unspoiled beach which you may well have all to yourself. Coconut palms line the coast to Nagua, the provincial capital, and beyond. The road follows the coast, making it a beautiful drive through the tropical landscape.

THE SAMANÁ PENINSULA

This finger of land, which sticks out to the east of the country, used to be an island until the 19th century when the bay began to silt up and land formed to join the two parts. The narrow channel where pirates used to hide has disappeared completely. A forested, hilly ridge runs down the peninsula, and the coastline is indented with picturesque bays. The best beaches are on the northern coast but the southern coast has the great attraction of whale watching: from January to March humpbacks migrate to the Bay of Samaná to mate or calve *(see page 72)*. Hotels are generally small and intimate with only a few all-inclusive hotels of moderate size so far, but things are changing with the construction of an international airport on the peninsula to encourage mass tourism. Hotels, condos, a marina and a golf course are all in the works.

Santa Bárbara de Samaná

Samaná is a pleasant town on the bay of the same name, set in a harbour protected by a few small islands. The two main cays are joined to the mainland by a causeway and add interest to the view from the Malecón, a broad waterfront drive running the length of the town. This is where people come to sit on a bench and contemplate the water, to promenade in the evening, and to party at night when there is a fiesta – or just at weekends when stalls are set up to sell food and drink.

Although the town was founded in 1756, evidence of its history is minimal because of a fire in 1946 and nearly all the buildings date from the second half of the 20th century, typically square blocks with a generous use of concrete. One of the oldest buildings is '**La Churcha**', which has an interesting history. In the 1820s, hundreds of freed slaves were brought from Philadelphia to settle here. They were known as Los Ingleses because they spoke English and had English names, which are still common in Samaná today. The Methodist Church in England raised money to build a church for them, which was sent out from England and erected on the hillside. Although rather dilapidated now, the white church with a red corrugated roof has been instrumental in maintaining many local customs, including the celebration of

'La Churcha' in Samaná

Harvest Festivals, which take place between the end of August and the end of October.

Most activity in town is seen around the docks, where the ferry boat leaves for Sabana de la Mar on the other side of the bay and from where boats for whale watching (see below) or trips along the coast to Los Haitises depart. Across

Whale Watching

For sheer exhilaration nothing beats seeing a huge, 40-ton humpback whale heaving itself out of the sea and throwing itself down again with an almighty splash. Technically known as 'breaching' these acrobatics are characteristic of humpbacks, which are the most energetic of whales. Samaná Bay is one of the best places in the world to see these magnificent mammals as it is estimated that around 300 of them are resident in the peak breeding time of February, with anything up to 1,500 cruising the area between January and March.

Humpbacks feed in the cold waters of the North Atlantic but migrate to the warmer waters of the Caribbean to give birth and provide the babies with a head start in life. During this time the young suckle and gain weight at a rate of 45kg (100lb) a day, but the mother will not feed until she migrates north again. The Dominican Republic has recently declared 24,000 sq km (9,250 sq miles) of water where they congregate to mate and calve a protected area, including the Banco de la Plata and Banco Navidad as well as Samaná Bay.

There are strict rules about whale watching in the bay, with permits granted to only 40 vessels, some large and some small (yolas). Boats have to take it in turns to approach whales near the surface, stay for a limited period of time and maintain a regulation distance. In addition, there are speed restrictions and no one is allowed in the water with whales. On a bigger boat you will be higher up and get a better view, as well as being able to stay longer out on the water and probably have the benefit of a naturalist on board.

the road are tour operators and restaurants. At the far end of the bay in an area called Tiro Blanco there is a small museum and the offices of the local conservation organisation, CEBSE, and the National Parks. The **museum** (Mon–Fri 9am–5pm; charge) has exhibits on flora and fauna, history and culture as well as the skeletons of a whale and a dolphin.

Cayo Levantado

Offshore to the east of the town is **Cayo Levantado**, also known as Bacardi Island, which is visited by tour boats because of the huge sweep of white sand at the west end of the island – an advertiser's dream. Tourists are deposited here for a swim and picnic lunch but you can also get a regular taxi boat from the Samaná dock. A new hotel on the island has marred the 'desert island' atmosphere.

Parque Nacional Los Haitises

Across the bay from the Samaná peninsula is the 208 sq km (80 sq mile) empty wilderness of **Los Haitises National Park**. The park, which has been protected since 1976, contains red, black and white mangroves, which are a nursery for all manner of aquatic and bird life, and a large area of humid sub-tropical forest. Its distinguishing characteristic is the number of *mogotes*, flat-topped hills caused by the uplifting and subsequent erosion of the limestone bedrock. It is believed that the limestone, originally from coral, formed 25 million years ago at the bottom of the sea, emerging 1.8 million years ago. Karst, which occurs when exposed rock begins to break up and dissolve, began 1 million years ago and continues today. Much of the landscape just looks like bumpy green hills but there are several sheer sided *mogotes* looming up out of the sea which provide a spectacular home for frigate birds and *rey congo* (black-crowned night heron).

Caves have formed in the limestone, which the Taínos used for shelter. They left behind them drawings and carvings in the rock which can still be clearly seen today with a flash light. There are bats in the caves and manatee and turtles in the mangroves, while a large number of birds can be spotted: herons, kingfishers, pelicans, frigate birds, terns, owls, hawks, todies, hummingbirds and swallows, among others, both migratory and resident.

A sheer-sided *mogote* in Los Haitises National Park

There are no roads, so access to the park is by boat from Sabana de la Mar, Sánchez or Samaná. Tour operators in Samaná usually send you by road to Sánchez, from where it is a shorter boat journey. Be prepared to get wet as the crossing is often rough and the boats are low in the water. Captains usually provide waterproof capes. Similarly, boat captains in Sabana de la Mar prefer to start from **Caño Hondo**, 10km (6 miles) from town along an appalling road, where there is a small pier on the river and the

National Park guards' station. It is only 15 minutes by boat from here to the caves, whereas it takes an hour from the town.

Las Terrenas

Las Terrenas, on the north side of the peninsula, is a charming, low-key village blessed with a long stretch of sandy beach which has been attracting visitors for years, particularly from Europe and Canada. Many French Canadians, Swiss, Spanish and others have never left,

preferring to set up home here and run businesses such as hotels and guesthouses, restaurants and tour companies. Difficult to get to, it was originally a backpacker's hideaway, but the advent of a paved road over the mountains, an airstrip and the new international airport have brought more people with more money. There are still cheap lodgings, but you can also find more upmarket places to stay.

There are lovely beaches all along this part of the coast. You can walk west from Las Terrenas along to **Playa Bonita**, where there are more low-rise hotels and restaurants under the palm trees. Further still is **Playa Cosón**, a largely deserted 6km (4-mile) long beach, except for guests at a new all-inclusive resort which has been built here. Access to the beach is tricky since its construction, but no beach is private in the Dominican Republic. Grandiose plans for a marina, golf course and villas will change the ecology as well as the character of the area in due course.

The upper falls of Salto El Limón

Salto El Limón

El Limón waterfall was made a National Monument in 1996 and makes for a lovely excursion into remote countryside. There are four access paths from the road between Las Terrenas and Samaná, from the villages of Rancho Español, Arroyo Surdido, El Café and El Limón. Horses and guides (obligatory) are for hire at many points along the road. You can hike if you prefer, like the guides do, but you will have to cross rivers and the track is often wet and muddy as well as steep, so take appropriate footwear. It takes about half an hour to ride through the forest to a lookout point on top of a hill the other side of the river from the waterfall. The view over the peninsula and down to the sea is stupendous. From here it's a 15-minute walk down to the river (take care – it is rocky and slippery). There are in fact two falls, the upper one is the most spectacular, although the quantity of water varies according to the time of year. In December the whole rock face is covered in water but at other times it looks more like white hair falling into the pool below. When it has rained the pool can be muddy, but once it has had a chance to settle it is clear. Take your swimsuit for a refreshing dip.

Las Galeras

At the eastern end of the north coast of the peninsula is **Playa Galeras**, where a fishing village has become a desirable place to stay. As in Las Terrenas, there are many foreign-run small hotels and guesthouses, although the village is smaller. The beautiful beach stretches for 1km (⅔ mile) between the dark cliffs of Cabo Cabrón and Cabo de Samaná, with forest stretching up the hillsides behind. It's quiet and peaceful, a perfect place to relax. The diving is excellent, with good coral in the bay and several sites around the rocky headland.

Further west along the bay, just under Cabo Cabrón, is **Playa Rincón**, a lovely, empty beach fringed with thousands of coconut palms reached either by boat or by an 8km (5-mile) road and then rough track from Las Galeras. The water is clear and good for swimming, with less coral and weed than at Las Galeras. There are other deserted beaches along this coast, many of them accessible only by sea. Take advice before swimming, however, as there is a strong undertow in places and people have drowned. **Playa El Valle** is a beautiful beach with no facilities except a basic beach bar. It is reached by boat taxi or by a 10km (6-mile) dirt road from Samaná involving two river crossings, so a 4WD is essential.

Some beaches are almost empty

WHAT TO DO

SPORTS

The Dominican Republic is ideal for those who like to be active. Whether on land or in the water there are plenty of adventure sports to keep anyone busy. The mountains are a playground for hikers or cyclists, the rivers lend themselves to rafting, kayaking and other extreme sports, while the sea offers excellent conditions for windsurfing as well as delights underwater for scuba divers. Dominicans mostly reserve their energies for baseball, and a visit to a match is an exciting way to get to know the people.

Hiking can be enjoyed in the many National Parks around the country. The most popular destination is Pico Duarte *(see page 54)*, the tallest mountain in the Caribbean. The trail to the top leads you through different ecosystems and you don't get much closer to nature than this. To enter a National Park you must pay a small fee and hire a local guide. Many guides speak only Spanish, so make sure you choose carefully. Organised group hiking is offered in Jarabacoa by Rancho Baiguate, a hotel and adventure sports centre (tel: 809 574 4940; www.ranchobaiguate.com). On the north coast trips are organised by Iguana Mama in Cabarete (tel: 809 571 0908; www.iguanamama.com). These companies will arrange guides, food and all camping equipment, so all you need to do is turn up with a good pair of boots and clothes to suit wet or dry conditions.

Mountain biking is very rewarding, with an extensive network of dirt tracks, trails and mule paths to get you into the countryside. If cycling uphill is not your strength, you can book a half day downhill tour and just enjoy free wheeling down with the wind in your face and the coast at your feet.

Serious cyclists, however, can go from coast to coast, up over the Cordillera Central using quiet roads which motorists complain are in poor condition but which are perfect for mountain bikes. There are now several places to hire bikes if you don't want to take your own, but Iguana Mama *(see page 79)* is the best and longest established company with professional equipment and guides.

River sports are excellent on the many rivers, gorges, waterfalls and rapids around Jarabacoa, and this town is now the centre of adventure tourism. November to May is the best and most exciting time of year because the rivers swell and flow faster in winter, but it can be done at any time of year. **Rafting** is mostly on the River Yaque del Norte, which is a level 3–4, with rocks and boulders to nego-tiate as well as rapids and gorges. **Tubing** is best in the wet season when you are less likely to bump into rocks. **Canyoning** is usually on the River Jimenoa, unless the river is too full and danger-ous, where there are caves, tunnels and waterfalls. **Cas-cading** can be done at any of the large waterfalls, such as El Salto de Baiguate in the Jarabacoa area and others around the country. **Kayak-ing** is on offer for beginner to advanced level, depending on the river. Beginners are

Rafting on the River Yaque del Norte

usually taken to the lower reaches of the River Yaque del Sur, which is class 2, then you progress to the middle Yaque or lower Jimenoa rivers, which are class 3. More advanced kayakers head for the upper Yaque for class 4 rapids and to the upper Jimenoa for class 5 and above, where there are waterfalls, drops, under-water staircases and other hazards to negotiate. The

Whale watching is another option, see page 72

main companies offering river sports are Aventura Máxima, owned by Rancho Baiguate (see page 79), and Iguana Mama (see page 79).

Horse riding is pleasurable out in the beautiful country-side as you make your way along picturesque trails through farms and forests, stopping to cool off in waterfalls and pools. The best riding is on the north coast in the foothills of the mountains, but even in out of the way resorts like Punta Cana there is good riding along the beach or under the stars at night. Wherever you go, make sure you check your horse and complain if it has sores where its harness rubs or it is lame. It is important that the saddle be comfortable for both you and the horse. Take local advice. Rancho Baiguate and Iguana Mama can give recommendations.

Golf is big business in the Dominican Republic, with more golf courses than any other Caribbean country. Several are of championship standard, built by top designers. Nearly all are attached to large hotels and you can get package deals. Casa de Campo, near La Romana, now has three golf courses, all of world class standard; the Punta Cana/Bávaro

Baseball is the national sport

area has several new and challenging courses by the sea; Playa Dorada's hotels were designed around the golf course; the Barceló resort complex at Bávaro has one hotel especially for golfers, while Playa Grande near Río San Juan is considered one of the most beautiful courses in the world with ten of its holes on top of the cliffs by the sea. Wherever you stay in the east or on the north coast, there will be a good golf course not far away. See www.dr1.com/golf for course reviews.

Scuba diving and **snorkelling** are excellent in most places around the coast with a healthy reef and plenty of colourful fish. On the north coast at Sosúa there is a PADI five-star dive resort, Northern Coast Aquasports/Diving, who have a good reputation for service and safety (tel: 809 571 1028; www.northerncoastdiving.com). Many of their dive sites are suitable for snorkelling or beginners. At Río San Juan by the Laguna Gri Grí you can visit a variety of beautiful underwater sites including caves, a wall and underwater mountains called the Seven Hills. In the east, at Bayahibe, there is spectacular diving in the Parque Nacional del Este, particularly around the little islands offshore, and there is the wreck of a large steel freighter to add variety. There are lots of fish as well as eels, rays, turtles, sharks and dolphins. The hotels have their own dive shops, but for independent travellers the best place to go is Scubafun (tel: 809 833 0003; www.scubafun.info).

Windsurfing is offered at most beach resorts, but is best at Cabarete where wind conditions are world class. International tournaments held here attract the very best windsurfers and during Cabarete Race Week the place is packed with professional and amateur racers. There are many windsurf schools all along the beach offering lessons and equipment hire, including Carib Bic Centre, Fanatic, Vela/Spinout and Natalie Simon. **Kitesurfing** is another exciting sport in the Cabarete area. It takes place west of the windsurfers for the sake of safety and presents a spectacular sight if you look

Baseball Mania

Baseball is the national sport. All small boys dream of becoming a star and a surprising number of Dominicans do make the grade. There is so much talent that several US and Canadian teams maintain feeder academies here and around 300–400 professional players in the USA come from the Dominican Republic. Sammy Sosa is a national hero, one of many who have become superstars. Born into poverty in San Pedro de Macorís, he beat the world batting record in 1998 and is now a multimillionaire with a charitable foundation which he uses partly to benefit his home town.

Going to a baseball match is an exciting experience as the crowd is very knowledgeable and partisan. The season runs from the last Friday in October to the end of December. Then in January the Serie Final is held, with semi-finals and finals to find the champion team *(campeón)*. After that the best players are selected for the national team to play in the Serie del Caribe in February, a regional tournament which the Dominican Republic usually wins. There are stadia at Santo Domingo, Santiago, San Pedro de Macorís and San Francisco de Macorís and five teams currently compete in the national league.

Baseball vocabulary is American but Hispanicised, so a baseball pitch is known as a *play de beisbol* and a home run is a *jonron*.

along the coast in the afternoons. Kitesurfing schools in Cabarete include Kitexcite (www.kitexcite.com).

ENTERTAINMENT

Dominicans have a strong sense of music and rhythm and are never short of enthusiasm to dance the night away. In the capital the best **discos** are in the top international hotels heading west along the Malecón, but there are other clubs and bars where you can hear live or recorded music and get on the dance floor. Elsewhere nightlife usually revolves around the town disco or hotel nightclub.

Merengue

Merengue can trace its origins back to the 19th century when workers developed their own dance for couples, with African influences mixing with the European styles that the upper classes favoured. The Haitian version is called *mereng* or *méringue* and the intermingling of folk music between the two countries made it unpopular with the elite. There were traditionally four musicians, who played the *cuatro* (like a guitar), the *güira* (a cylindrical scraper), the *tambora* (a two headed drum) and the *marimba* (a wooden box with plucked metal keys). While the guitar shows the Spanish heritage, the percussion instruments owe their origin to Africa and it is percussion which gives merengue its characteristic rhythm. There were, however, regional variations. In the Cibao Valley, where there were many German tobacco and sugar merchants in the 19th century, the accordion was introduced instead of the güira. In the mid-20th century when big bands were popular, the saxophone, trumpet or trombone were tried, while later on even the electric bass guitar was added. The typical merengue song starts with a short introduction, *paseo*, before going into the main lyrics which would often have a topical relevance or social comment, followed by a call and response section, *jaleo*.

The heady combination of African beat and Latin sensuality has evolved over time into the **merengue**, a fast but simple two-step dance which Dominicans make into something unbelievably sexy by rotating their hips in time with the music. Children instinctively follow the beat, but Europeans and North Americans have trouble with their inhibitions and are generally fairly wooden. The music is heard everywhere: on buses, in bars, cafés and discos, and it's definitely the national dance. The popularity of merengue has spread with Dominicans across the

Dominicans love their music

water to the United States, and many of the big recording artists now work from there, helping to give the music worldwide appeal.

The other popular style of music is **bachata**. This evolved as a sentimental genre with a male singer bemoaning his unrequited love or a betrayal, but became hugely popular when Juan Luis Guerra, one of the leading Dominican crooners, experimented and turned it into romantic poetry. His already large female audience lapped it up and it now rivals merengue in the nation's affections. Bachata songs derive from the same roots as boleros with the guitar, the rhythm and the sentimental lyrics, but are faster, with one singer instead of three.

Cabaret dancer

Casinos are very popular and most large hotels offer banks of gaming machines and gambling tables. Santo Domingo has around ten casinos and there are others on the north coast in Playa Dorada and in the east at Bávaro. **Cabaret** and **dance shows** are often staged in conjunction with the casinos – they don't quite come up to Las Vegas standards, but are entertaining nonetheless. An interesting dance show, for its location, if nothing else, is the *Guácara Taína* in Santo Domingo. Shows of supposedly Taíno dancing are staged in an enormous cave, complete with stalactites and pictographs, and there are two dance floors where they play all types of music for dancing after the show. Avenida Mirador del Sur, tel: 809 530 2666; Tue–Sun, 5pm–2am.

The best **theatres** for concerts, opera, ballet and drama are the Teatro Nacional in the Plaza de la Cultura, Santo Domingo, and the modern theatre in Santiago. **Cinemas** are American style multiplex affairs showing Hollywood or action movies. The latest to be built in Santo Domingo is an enormous 10-screen cinema in a mall appropriately called the Megacentro, which takes up two blocks on the east side of the river at the junction of Mella and San Vicente. There are also cinemas in Santiago and in Playa Dorada.

SHOPPING

There is no shortage of souvenirs to take home and good deals in amber, larimar and other jewellery can be found everywhere. The country is world famous for its cigars, which can be accompanied by some excellent aged rum. There is a good variety of high-quality handicrafts and art, although, as anywhere, there is also a lot of rubbish sold.

Amber is found in the mountains behind Puerto Plata. The colour varies according to age, while most pieces contain streaks and dirt. The best pieces, commanding the highest prices, have insects or leaves trapped in the resin. Amber can be found set in gold or silver in a range of modern or traditional designs.

Most of the top hotels have elegant jewellery shops where you can purchase amber, but the amber museums also have excellent shops. In Santo Domingo go to the **Museo Mundo de Ambar** (Arzobispo Meriño 452 esquina Restauración; Mon–Sat 9am–6pm). In Puerto Plata there is the **Museo del Ambar** (Duarte 61 esquina Emilio Prud'homme; daily 9am–5pm; *see page 64*). The museum has another shop in the Playa Dorada shopping centre (daily 8am–10pm).

Larimar is a cool blue semi-precious stone of volcanic origin and, like amber, is widely available throughout the country. It was first commercialised by Miguel Méndez and a Peace Corps Volunteer, Norman Rilling, in 1974. They named it after Méndez' daughter, Larisa, and the blue sea *(mar)*, as

Amber rules

Be sure you are not tricked into buying plastic – imitation amber is extremely sophisticated. Remember that real amber fluoresces under ultraviolet light and reputable shops will have a UV light available for testing. It also floats in salt water while plastic will sink, and produces static electricity when rubbed.

the stones were first found on the beach. Nowadays it comes from mountain deposits southwest of Barahona. At the **Larimar Museo Dominicano** (Isabel La Católica, Santo Domingo; daily 9am–5pm), you can visit the museum upstairs reached by a staircase with lovely larimar handrails, and buy uncut or polished stones and jewellery downstairs, in a shop with counter tops in larimar. Alternatively, for uncut stones you can go to the mines in the Barahona area *(see page 46)*. The museum is small, but well laid out with good descriptions of the stone's volcanic origins (www. larimarmuseum.com).

Cigars Tobacco has been grown here for centuries, since the Taínos introduced it to the Spanish. Columbus noted how the Amerindians puffed on smoking rolls of leaves and appeared to hallucinate with them on ceremonial occasions. The Spaniards soon picked up the habit and demand remains high today. The Dominican Republic claims better quality than Cuba, its major competitor. They are still hand made by traditional methods and workers roll the dried leaves to age-old recipes. Quality control is rigidly enforced and a team of inspectors checks every single cigar. If you're interested in visiting a factory, *see page 60*.

Cigars are still rolled by hand

Rum is drunk widely and some is of excellent quality. The best of the brand names are Brugal, Barceló and Bermúdez, although there are many others on the supermarket shelves. Light rum *(blanco)* is young, dry and usually mixed with a fruit punch or other mixer such as cola. Golden rum (*amarillo*) is aged for a year in a barrel and has a better flavour, while dark rum (*añejo*) is aged for several years and is usually drunk neat or on the rocks like a good malt whisky.

Coffee is grown on the lower slopes of the mountains and mostly exported to Europe for blending, but there is plenty on the domestic market. *Café Santo Domingo* is one of the better brands and can be bought at the airport if you've still got room in your hand luggage.

A matter of taste: local naïf art has endlessly repeated themes

Art is pushed under your nose at every corner, but most is imitation Haitian naïf art and not of good quality. It is bright and colourful but the themes are repeated endlessly as artists copy each other and reproduce what they think is popular. Nevertheless, there are some excellent painters and sculptors in the Dominican Republic whose work can be found in serious galleries away from the tourist hustle. Art in the Dominican Republic only started to develop a national identity in the 20th century, so to find out what you like, the **Museo de Arte Moderno in the Plaza de Cultura** (Modern Art Museum; *see page 32)* is an excellent place to start.

Ceramics with Taíno motifs

Handicrafts fill the shelves of gift shops and all sorts of ceramics, weavings, basket ware and carvings vie for your attention. Of interest are the carvings from the guayacán tree, an ancient gnarled wood which is surprisingly heavy and multicoloured. To bombard your senses go to the **Mercado Modelo** in Santo Domingo, where dozens of stallholders compete for your custom. It is interesting to browse and get a feel for what is on offer, including some *vodú* items and the alleged aphrodisiac drink called *mamajuana*, which is a rum infused with herbs, bark and various substances. Note that if you go with a guide and you buy something, he will get a commission and your price is inflated by an equivalent amount. Bargaining is expected.

CHILDREN'S DR

The Dominican Republic is an ideal family destination and perfect for a beach holiday. The sea is warm, clear and unpolluted with no nasty surprises such as stinging jelly fish, sea urchins or sharks. Most hotels have pools in case the sea is rough. There is plenty of sand to play on and usually palm trees for shade. However, the sun is fierce from about 10am until 4pm so small children should be well covered up and you will need a large quantity of high factor sun cream for the whole family. Don't be fooled by the cooling breeze, you may not feel hot but children will burn.

Most of the beach hotels are all-inclusives and will lay on entertainment for children of all ages.

Away from the beach there are lots of activities, especially if you are on the north coast where things are more convenient. Iguana Mama in Cabarete *(see page 79)* runs cycling tours designed for families, with bikes of all sizes and lots of back up. Horse riding can be enjoyed by all as the horses are quiet and small, and it is a good way of introducing children to the Dominican countryside.

Teenagers over 14 will get a thrill out of whitewater rafting at Jarabacoa and will probably enjoy a baseball match. Sightseeing excursions are usually fine for kids, particularly the safari trips which use jeeps or military vehicles, although some cover large distances and you may be some hours travelling.

Horse riding is ideal for youngsters

If you're visiting between January and March, don't miss the opportunity to take your children whale watching at Samaná *(see page 72)*. Choose a large boat, such as Victoria Marine, run by Kim Beddall, of Whale Samaná (tel: 809 538 2494) as not only does she hand out sea sickness pills, but the guides are naturalists and the trips are more educational than on the smaller boats where you get pitched around on the waves.

Festivals

There are lots of festivals, whether religious, cultural or sporting, and Dominicans don't need much of an excuse to have a party. Merengue is so popular that it has its own festivals. Santo Domingo holds a merengue festival in July, Sosúa has one in September and Puerto Plata in October, all with associated exhibitions and activities such as gastronomy or handicrafts.

New Year Year-end celebrations run from 22 December to 2 January, with New Year's Eve festivities on the Malecón in Santo Domingo, a huge outdoor disco with bands playing. The party ends in a blaze of fireworks.

21 January Our Lady of Altagracia, in honour of the spiritual mother of the country. All-night vigils *(velaciones)*, with music and singing followed by religious processions, take place in several towns. The largest is probably at Higüey cathedral, the destination of a mass pilgrimage for several days beforehand, where the surrounding park and streets become an enormous market and outdoor party the night of 20 January.

End February Carnival, coinciding with Independence Day on 27 February. Each town has its own method of celebrating, sometimes for several weeks in advance (www.carnaval.com.do). The elaborate costumes are based on historical, religious or mythological characters. It's worth visiting the Museo del Hombre Dominicano *(see page 32)*, to see the exhibition of masks *(caretas)* and costumes. In Santo Domingo parades take place along the Malecón. In Santiago there is a central character, the piglet, which represents the devil, while in Monte Cristi they have mock battles between the *toros* (bulls) and the *civiles* (civilians) and in La Vega dancers wear masks of the devil *(diablos cojuelos)* and wield balls on ropes *(vejigas)* with which they try and hit people.

Easter Semana Santa (Holy Week) is a holiday everywhere with religious processions and other festivities.

16 August Restoration Day, a national holiday with more carnival parades.

June Festival Presidente de Música Latina, including music from the Caribbean and Central America.

July Merengue festival in Santo Domingo. Dozens of merengue bands perform in hotels, on the Malecón, Avenida del Puerto and in Boca Chica.

EATING OUT

The typical Dominican meal is not a great culinary experience but is usually tasty and could be classified as 'comfort food', being heavily based on carbohydrates from the days when slaves needed lots of calories. As a sugar producing country, there is also considerable use of sugar and desserts are unbelievably sweet. Food is nearly always freshly cooked and Dominican housewives or maids traditionally shop daily for their needs. They buy in small amounts, often from the corner shop (colmado), a treasure trove of dried goods and rum. Fruit and vegetables are bought when in season from street sellers or market stalls. For cordon bleu cooking you need to pick a good hotel with foreign investment or find a similar restaurant in Santo Domingo. There are several excellent Spanish restaurants, and lots of other nationalities are represented, including the USA with their fast food chains.

Fruit can be bought from street sellers

Meal Times

Dominicans like to eat three good meals a day, starting with a cooked breakfast (desayuno) from 7 to 9am. Lunch (almuerzo) in restaurants is usually served from around noon to 1pm and dinner/supper (comida/cena) from 6 to 10pm. Some restaurants offer all-day service, not closing between meals, and there are plenty of cafés for snacks and

Fresh fish is widely available

sandwiches. Dominicans frequently snack between meals and can not go long without a shot of strong, sweet, black coffee *(cafecito)*, sold on the streets in thimble-sized measures.

What to Eat

The traditional dish is known as *la bandera Dominicana*, the Dominican flag, because of the combination of colours. It consists of stewed beef, rice and red kidney beans and can be accompanied by seasonal salads such as avocado or with a serving of fried plantains. Dominicans eat this, or similar, *comida criolla*, for lunch nearly every day, varying the types of meat, beans and accompaniments. However, they consider they have not eaten properly if they have not had rice and beans. If you eat in a local restaurant *(comedor)*, you choose the meat you want and how you want it cooked (stewed, roasted, fried) and the rice, beans, salad, plantain, sweet potato or yuca come as standard. Portions are generous, particularly of rice, and prices are moderate to cheap depending on your location.

Other *comida criolla* dishes include *sancocho* or *salcocho prieto*, a slightly spicy stew of up to seven different types of meat and vegetables, while *mondongo* is tripe stew. *Mofongo* is a spicy stew with chunks of plantain in it and there are several restaurants in Santo Domingo which specialise in it. *Locrio* is a rice dish with meat, chicken or sausages, not to be confused with *asopao*, which is somewhere between a soup and a risotto with fish or chicken. Goat meat is common, usually either roast *(chivo asado)*, having been marinated in herbs, lime juice and garlic, or stewed *(chivo guisado)*. Other common meats are beef, pork and chicken, while rabbit and guinea fowl are eaten in the mountains. All cuts of meat are used and bones are left in. It is not considered bad manners to pick up the bones with your fingers and paper napkins and toothpicks are provided on the table.

Plenty of **fish** is available round the coast and even some fresh water fish can be found inland. There are many different varieties, but if you eat in a *comedor* it will be unspecified and simply referred to as 'fish'. You can have it fried *(frito)*, grilled *(a la plancha)*, in a tomato sauce *(a la criolla)* or cooked in coconut milk *(al coco)*. Stalls set up on the beach at weekends sell freshly fried fish with an array of side dishes – all fried – such as plantain, yuca or sweet potato.

Salads served as an accompaniment to the main meal usually include shredded cabbage or lettuce, tomato, cucumber and avocado when in season. Sometimes you may be offered Russian salad, a mixture of cooked potato and other vegetables swamped with mayonnaise.

Fresh tropical fruits, cereals, yoghurt, bread (banana bread is moist and delicious) and pastries are available in the mornings, washed down with juices and coffee, but a cooked **breakfast** can be an elaborate affair. Apart from eggs you may be offered local sausages *(longaniza)*, fish, potatoes, bacon and *mangú*. This is mashed plantain mixed with onion and oil, a filling dish to start the day.

For a less substantial breakfast Dominicans often eat *yaniqueque* with hot chocolate or milky coffee. There are many versions of 'Johnny Cake' throughout the Caribbean islands, dating from the days of slavery, but this one is made from a paste of wheat flour and water, rolled out like a pancake and deep fried until it puffs up and turns golden and crispy. You can also find it served as a snack on the beach, usually dusted with salt for flavour. Other **snacks** found on the street include *pastelitos* (pasties filled with minced beef, chicken or cheese) or *quipes* (cracked wheat fritters with a meat filling), both fried while you wait. Instead of potato crisps you can find *platanitos*, thinly sliced and fried plantain dusted with salt, or *tostones*, which are thickly sliced and fried twice.

Fruit is out of this world, with a wide range of tropical fruits available at every meal but particularly breakfast. Hotel buffets usually include pineapple *(piña)*, melon, mango, banana *(guineo)*, papaya *(lechoza)* and a range of citrus fruits such as grapefruit or orange (not the seedless variety).

Tostones

Tostones are crisp slices of plantain served as an accompaniment to a main meal or sometimes on their own with a drink.

Slice the plantains into 2-cm/1-inch slices and soak in salt water for 20 minutes in the fridge. Drain and dry on paper towels. Shallow fry (1 cm/½ inch oil) on both sides for 2 minutes until they start to turn colour. Drain and dry on paper towels then flatten with a plate, rolling pin or similar. Fry again for about 5 minutes until golden and crispy. Drain, dry, dust with salt and serve.

Elsewhere you can find more unusual fruits such as soursop *(guanábana)*, passion fruit *(granadilla)*, mammee apple *(mamey)*, custard apple *(chirimoya* or *jaguey)*, guava *(guayaba)* or *limoncillo*, a small, round, green fruit which grows in bunches rather like oversized grapes. These are often sold by street traders in towns or on the side of the road in areas where they are grown and where they are cheaper.

Desserts are unbelievably sweet. Dominicans happily chew on a length of sugar cane and expect a generous amount of sugar in their puddings. The

Banana crop

sweetest of all is *dulce de leche*, a combination of sugar and condensed milk, boiled to caramel consistency and flavoured with vanilla, coconut, cocoa, fruit or anything else. Fruit is often preserved and served in a sugar syrup you could stand a spoon in. Alternatives include gateaux covered in frosted icing, very sticky and colourful. Less sweet and usually delicious is *flan* (crème caramel), or you may find a fresh fruit salad.

What to Drink

Fruit juices are tempting although hotels usually serve the pasteurised variety rather than fresh. In cafés you can find many varieties of juice *(jugo)*, liquidised fruit *(licuado)* or fruit milk shake *(batido)*. It is best to specify how much sugar you like, if any. Sorrel is made from the sepals of the sorrel flower which have been steeped in water and other flavourings to make a red, bitter drink, that certainly makes a change from sugary juices on offer. Tamarind is another refreshing soft drink, made from the pulp surrounding the seeds in the tamarind pod, and a fresh lemonade can't be beaten on a hot sunny day.

There are lots of **soft drinks** sold in bottles or cans and referred to as *refrescos*. Most of the American brand names are available as well as several locally produced fizzy drinks which come in a variety of flavours.

Dominicans drink a lot of **beer**, which is usually sold in bottles, although cans are also available. The leading brand name is Presidente, which dominates the market through extensive advertising and sponsorship. It is a lager beer

Presidente dominates the beer market

and the bottles come in three sizes, small (an individual serving), large (enough for three glasses) and 1 litre. Other beer brand names are Quisqueya and Bohemia, which are less widespread. Dark beer is available, but the enormous fridges you see in bars and *colmados* are usually full of Presidente. Heineken is made under licence by the same company that makes Presidente.

Rum is the main spirit because it is distilled here and is cheap, although imported gin and whisky are also found on supermarket shelves. Brand names include Barceló (60 percent market share), Brugal (30 percent), Bermúdez and any number of others selling a range of white, amber or aged rum *(see Shopping, page 88)*. A look around a *colmado* reveals a huge range of sizes of bottles, but if you are in a club or disco ask for a *servicio*, and you will get a ⅕-litre bottle of rum with a bucket of ice and *refrescos*. If you don't want to smother your rum in fruit juice or Coca Cola, go for a Special Reserve or a Gran Añejo, as good as a brandy. Nearly all **cocktails** are rum-based and it can be fun working your way through the barman's list if you've got the stamina. Piña colada is always on the menu, often served in a pineapple or coconut with all the trimmings, and several flavours of daiquirí are usually on offer. Rum punch tends to be rather sweet but each barman has his own

Water

Bottled water is widely available and recommended. Dominicans buy large containers of drinking water and if a jug of water is placed on the table it will probably be from one of these and not from the tap. You can always ask for a bottle of water if you prefer. Avoid tap water, which has not been purified for drinking, unless you are in a hotel where you are specifically advised that it is safe because they have their own purification system.

Rum for sale

recipe and selection of fruit juices, so it is worth trying.

Wine is not local to the Dominican Republic and is always imported. A lot of it comes from Chile and is reliable, but watch out for the house wine served at dinner in all-inclusive hotels; much of it is disgusting.

Coffee is grown in the mountains and Dominicans drink lots of it. The best places to get good coffee are in cafeterías, *comedores*, or even from street vendors, who make strong black espresso-type coffee. Hotels often ruin their coffee, which can be weak and/or bitter, and is not improved with the addition of milk.

To Help You Order…

Could we have a table?	**Queremos una mesa**
Do you have a set menu?	**¿Tiene un menú del día?**
The menu, please	**La carta, por favor**
I want a/an/some	**Quiero…**
The bill, please	**La cuenta, por favor**

bread	**pan**	pepper	**pimiento**
butter	**mantequilla**	potatoes	**papa**
coffee	**café/cafecito**	rice	**arroz**
dessert	**postre**	rum	**ron**
fish	**pescado**	salad	**ensalada**
fork	**tenedor**	salt	**sal**
fruit	**fruta**	sandwich	**bocadillo**

glass	**vaso/copa**	soup	**sopa**
ice cream	**helado**	sugar	**azúcar**
knife	**cuchillo**	tea	**té**
meat	**carne**	water	**agua**
milk	**leche**	wine	**vino**
spoon	**cuchara**	(white/red)	**(blanco/tinto)**

...and Read the Menu

aguacate	avocado	**habichuela**	beans
ají	chilli	**huevo**	egg
ajo	garlic	**jamón**	ham
bacalao	salt cod	**langosta**	lobster
berro	watercress	**limón**	lime
caldo	clear soup	**lomo de**	loin of
calamares	squid	**cerdo**	pork
callos	tripe	**longaniza**	sausage
camarones	prawns	**mariscos**	seafood
casabe	cassava/	**merluza**	hake
	yuca bread	**mero**	grouper
cazuela/	casserole/	**naranja**	orange
zarzuela	stew	**pavo**	turkey
cebolla	onion	**pescado**	fish
chillo	red snapper	**picante**	spicy
al coco	in coconut	**plátano**	plantain/
chivo	goat		green banana
chuleta	chop	**pollo**	chicken
conejo	rabbit	**pulpo**	octopus
crudo	raw	**queso**	cheese
filete	steak	**repollo**	cabbage
guarapa	sugar cane	**res**	beef
	juice	**salsa**	sauce
guinea	guinea fowl	**tayota**	christophene
guineo	sweet banana	**tostones**	plantain chips

HANDY TRAVEL TIPS

An A–Z Summary of Practical Information

A

ACCOMMODATION (See also CAMPING and the list of recommended HOTELS AND RESTAURANTS)

There is a wide range of places to stay, from basic family-run guest-houses to five-star hotels with every luxury. You can pay as little as US$15 or over US$150 a night for a room and the majority of hotels offer meal packages. Bed and breakfast, half board, full board and all-inclusive are available.

In Santo Domingo the international-style hotels are along the Malecón. They provide business centres, conference centres, swimming pools, restaurants, bars and entertainment such as casinos. More interesting and with more character are the renovated colonial buildings in the old city.

There are few luxury hotels in the mountains; instead you find pleasant country inns and guesthouses at rates that will not break the bank. They are generally friendly, family-run places that maintain a good level of comfort and are clean, quiet and relaxing, and helpful in arranging whatever activity you want to do.

The majority of hotel rooms are in beach resorts, concentrated on the north, the east and the southeast coasts. The remote nature of these resorts has led to the development of the all-inclusive concept as there is little alternative to eating in your hotel. Some hotels are massive, with thousands of rooms, and are like self-contained villages, but it is not impossible to find a small hotel on the beach – you just need to know where to look. The Samaná Peninsula, for example, still has intimate hotels and guesthouses, while others are still hanging on along the north coast. For visitors to the south and

I'd like a single/double room with bath/shower.
What's the rate per night?

**Quiero una habitación sencilla/doble con baño/ducha.
¿Cuál es el precio por noche?**

west coasts accommodation is sparse, and the lack of tourists means that standards are not quite so high.

All hotels charge 23 percent on top of the bill: 10 percent service and 13 percent sales tax.

AIRPORTS *(aeropuertos)* (See also GETTING THERE)

There are several international airports around the country, serving the capital, the north coast, the east and (potentially) the southwest. Santo Domingo's **Aeropuerto Las Américas** (tel: 809 549 0450) is 23km (14 miles) to the east of the city on the way to Boca Chica. When you arrive you will be greeted by long queues for tourist cards and immigration, so it is to your advantage to get your card in your home country before you travel. There are also phones, toilets and a tourist kiosk before immigration. There is a bank after Customs, along with loads of car hire offices. Upstairs in the departure area you'll find airlines, snack bars and gift shops and once through passport control there are lots of duty-free shops in the departure lounge.

Taxis wait just outside Customs and cost US$20–25 into the capital or US$10–15 to Boca Chica. Calling a radio taxi on your return will save you about a third of the price. The journey can take as little as half an hour, but allow an hour for heavy traffic. Alternatively, upstairs in the departure area are *colectivo* taxis which leave when full, are much cheaper and have a set route into Santo Domingo. Buses pass the turnoff for the airport on the Santo Domingo–Boca Chica route, so if you are prepared to walk 1½km (1 mile) to the junction this is the cheapest method of getting to and from the airport. If you are driving back from Santo Domingo, remember that you will need RD$30 for the toll *(peaje)* on the *autopista*. Road construction works are in progress and driving into the city at night can be confusing.

On the north coast the **Gregorio Luperón** international airport is 15–20 minutes' drive from Puerto Plata, 10 minutes from Sosúa and 20 minutes from Cabarete. The airport is a reasonable size and there is a bank, car hire agencies and shops. Baggage handlers can be pushy and expect US$2 per bag. Taxis charge around US$25 to Puerto Plata or Cabarete and US$13 to Sosúa, but if you walk to the junction you can catch a bus going along the main road: Puerto Plata to your right, Sosúa and Cabarete to your left.

A new airport has been built at **La Romana**, principally serving Casa de Campo resort, but it is also close to Bayahibe and the hotels there. Flights tend to be seasonal and there are more charter than scheduled flights. The airport at **Punta Cana** serves the resorts in the far east of the island and most guests are shuttled to their hotels on buses, although expensive taxis and car hire are available. The airport at **Santiago de los Caballeros** is now being used for international flights. An international airport on the Samaná Peninsula, **Arroyo Barril**, was inadequate for long haul flights, but another airport opened in 2007 at the west end of the peninsula. In the southwest, **María Montéz** at Barahona is used only for domestic flights.

B

BICYCLE HIRE (RENTAL)

Many hotels rent bikes but they will not be state-of-the-art mountain bikes necessary for off road cycling. The best place to hire bikes or join a group tour is **Iguana Mama**, Calle Principal in Cabarete, tel: 809 571 0908; www.iguanamama.com, info@iguanamama.com.

BUDGETING FOR YOUR TRIP

With the depreciation of the peso, the Dominican Republic is cheaper than many other Caribbean destinations.

Transport to the Dominican Republic. There are regular scheduled services to Santo Domingo from The Netherlands, France, Germany and Spain but charter flights are available from many more European destinations including the UK. Scheduled flights booked in advance cost from US$550 but you can pick up a last minute bargain on the internet for around US$300. There are lots of scheduled flights from US cities and cheap deals can be picked up on the Miami, Fort Lauderdale or New York routes.

Accommodation. Room rates vary according to season, with the very highest prices at Christmas and Easter. High season is 15 December–15 April and low season, when rates are up to a third less, the rest of the year. Some hotels operate shoulder seasons as well, particularly all-inclusives. The top hotels can cost US$150–200 a night, but a good mid-range hotel will be US$30–60, with comfortable beds, private bathroom, TV, fan and/or air conditioning. A few luxuries or a particularly fine setting will push the price above US$60. For travellers on a low budget, there are basic places to stay for less than US$20, but you may not get hot water and security is not guaranteed.

Meals. Dinner for two in a posh restaurant in Santo Domingo will cost from US$70–100, depending on the wine chosen, but there are plenty of places where the main course will cost you US$10 or less. Lunch in a *comedor* in the capital costs US$4–6, twice what it will cost outside the capital including coffee and a beer. Most hotels offer meal plans which can be economical.

Local transport. Buses and *colectivos* are cheap, and taxis are reasonable. The price of fuel is rising so fares are going up. Urban bus fares are only a few pesos and a short taxi ride will cost you US$3–4. Motorbike taxis *(motoconchos)* cost less than a taxi but more than a bus. Long distance bus fares are also good value at around US$6 for a 4-hour journey.

Incidentals. Your major expenses will be excursions, entertainment and daytime sporting activities. A day trip involving transport, lunch and a guide costs US$35–45, but if you go on a boat or there is some sporting activity involved as well, the price rises to US$75 or more depending on how far you travel. Hiring a car allows maximum flexibility, particularly if you want to explore the coast or the mountains. Prices vary according to the company, time of week and season, but a car will cost US$35–60 a day, with discounts for longer hire. Premium unleaded fuel costs US$4.20, ordinary US$3.85 and diesel US$2.95

per US gallon. If you go on a toll road it will cost you RD$30 out of Santo Domingo, but this is a return charge and you pay nothing on the way back to the city. You need six RD$5 coins for the toll booth.

At night, entry to a club or disco costs US$2–12, depending on whether there is a live band playing or a show. Beer or rum is around US$2 but imported drinks cost more.

C

CAMPING

There are no campsites in the Dominican Republic. One or two hotels in the interior allow camping in their grounds and camping is permitted when hiking in the mountains in the National Parks with a guide.

CAR HIRE (RENTAL) (coches de alquiler) (See also DRIVING)

You must be 25, have a valid driving licence and a credit card to rent a vehicle for up to 90 days. There are both local and major international car rental agencies in Santo Domingo, at the airports and at the major beach resorts. Prices vary significantly so shop around. Generally a local company will be cheaper but they may not have the vehicle you want. Basic rates start at US$35–60, but can be as much as US$100 a day. Weekly rates are better value. Car hire companies include **Avis** (Sarasota y Lincoln, Santo Domingo, tel: 809 535 7191), **Dollar** (Avenida Independencia 366, Santo Domingo, tel: 809 221 7368), **Hertz** (airport, tel: 809 221 5333) and **MC Auto** (Avenida George Washington 105, Santo Domingo, tel: 809 688 6518).

I'd like to hire a car (tomorrow).	**Quiero alquilar un coche (para mañana).**
for one day/a week	**por un día/una semana**
Please include full insurance.	**Haga el favor de incluir el seguro a todo riesgo.**

CLIMATE

The climate is tropical and hot all year round. However, it is cooler and drier January–April than in the rest of the year. May and June can be wet, but short, sharp showers can be expected at any time of year. The average temperature is about 25°C (77°F), although it is much cooler in the mountains than down at sea level. The temperature falls an average of 6°C (11°F) for every 1,000m (3,000ft) of altitude above sea level and up on Pico Duarte and around Constanza there are occasional frosts. Some areas of the country are much drier than others, and parts of the southwest are almost deserts with scant rainfall.

In June the hurricane season officially begins and storms can blow up at any time. The worst hurricanes usually turn up between September and November and can cause major damage. A tropical storm is a system of strong thunderstorms with a defined circulation and maximum sustained winds of 39–73 mph (34–63 knots). A hurricane is more intense, with a well-defined circulation and winds of 74 mph (64 knots) or more. The authorities issue watches (36 hours before arrival) and warnings (24 hours) for both tropical storms and hurricanes.

CLOTHING

Tropical, light-weight clothing is best, but if you are going up into the mountains you will need a long sleeved top for the evenings and a fleece if you are camping out on Pico Duarte where it can get quite cold. Good boots are essential for hiking in the mountains and a waterproof jacket is recommended. Shorts and skimpy tops are fine at the beach, but cover up if you are going into town, particularly if visiting churches, when bare arms and legs are considered inappropriate. Dominicans dress up to go out at night and look smart and sexy. Men will probably not wear a tie to go to a restaurant, but they will to go to the theatre. Women wearing very brief outfits or lycra are likely to be prostitutes.

CRIME AND SAFETY (See also POLICE)

There is very little violent crime against tourists. However, as with any-where, you should guard against theft and take the usual precautions. Most of the better hotels offer a safe deposit box either in your room or at reception. Never flaunt your valuables in the street, keep jewellery discreet, hide your money and keep hold of cameras and bags. Never leave your possessions unattended on the beach. Do not walk the streets of Santo Domingo after 11pm – take a taxi instead. Report any crime to the police and get a statement for your insurance company.

I want to report a theft.	**Quiero denunciar un robo**
My handbag/ticket/wallet/ passport has been stolen	**Me han robado el bolso/el billete/la cartera/el pasaporte**
Help! Thief!	**¡Socorro! ¡Ladrón!**

CUSTOMS (aduana) AND ENTRY REQUIREMENTS

You need a passport and 90-day, US$10 tourist card to enter the country. The tourist card can be bought in advance from consulates, tourist offices and some airlines, but you can also buy it on arrival before going through immigration (be prepared to wait for up to an hour). All visitors should have a return or onward ticket.

Currency restrictions. You may not take currency in excess of US$10,000 out of the country. Keep your receipt when you exchange money; any surplus pesos can be exchanged at the end of your visit for up to 30 percent of the total bought. This does not apply to currency purchases on a credit card.

Customs. You may bring in 2 litres of alcoholic beverages, 200 cig-arettes and gifts to a value of US$1,000. Check the regulations of your own country before purchasing souvenirs and gifts to take home.

I have nothing to declare	**No tengo nada a declarar**

D

DRIVING

Not all Dominican drivers have licences and their driving can be erratic. Hand signals mean nothing in particular except that the driver is going to do something. Motorcyclists are all over the place and often do not wear helmets. A whole family can be carried on a motorbike, or a huge amount of equipment. It is not unusual to see something like a washing machine being carried strapped to the passenger seat. Inevitably they wobble around a lot. Avoid driving at night. Dominicans do not always have functioning headlights. Those who do rarely dip them until you are practically on top of them, or else flash them at you as you approach to let you know they are there. Animals on the road, potholes and poorly lit road works are additional hazards. There are many military checkpoints, particularly in the border areas with Haiti. Foreigners are not often stopped, but occasionally there is a sweep for drugs and arms and they stop everybody.

Road conditions. The main roads are in reasonable condition but a lot of building work is going on to improve access into and out of Santo Domingo and from the capital out to the regions, so be prepared for road works. Roads in rural areas are often unpaved or potholed. A four-wheel-drive vehicle is often needed to get to remote places, so check before you hire as there may be restrictions on where you can take a hire car. Animals tend to roam freely and it is not unusual to meet a herd of goats. People sell produce and other goods on the roadside, so you have to watch out for other drivers swerving on and off the road. Every town or village has speed bumps at the entrance and exit. These are usually painted yellow and white but the paint fades and they are not always visible. Take them very slowly and at an angle if possible as they are high. Equally difficult are storm drains in towns, often at traffic lights, again best negotiated diagonally.

Rules and regulations. Drive on the right, overtake on the left. However, on a dual carriageway such as the Autopista Duarte drivers go wherever they fancy and no one pays any heed to which is the fast lane and which is the slow lane. Speed limits are 40 km/h (25mph) in urban areas, 60 km/h (38mph) on suburban roads and 80 km/h (50mph) on main roads. There are visible signs, but Dominicans see these as a suggestion rather than a rule. Wear your seat belt and if you are on a motorcycle wear a helmet.

Fuel costs. Premium unleaded fuel costs US\$4.20, ordinary US\$3.85 and diesel US\$2.95 per US gallon. Not all filling stations are 24-hour. There are no self-service filling stations, you will always be served. Most take credit cards but cash is quicker.

Parking. Santo Domingo has little parking space in the centre and you are advised not to drive there as roads are narrow and a badly signed one-way system means that you are bound to go the wrong way and meet oncoming traffic. Supermarkets and shopping malls in the suburbs have car parks, otherwise you may find an empty parking place with an enterprising attendant who will mind your car for you. In other towns you will have to look for a parking space on the side of the road or an unofficial car park.

Road signs. Apart from the standard international pictographs, you may encounter the following:

No rebase	no overtaking
El muro/	speedbump/
policía acostado	sleeping policeman
Velocidad máxima	speed limit
Motoconcho	motorbike taxi
Doblar a la izquierda/derecha	turn left/right
Siga derecho	keep straight on
Combustible	fuel
Gasolina	petrol
Gasoil	diesel
Sin plomo	lead free

E

ELECTRICITY *(corriente eléctrica)*

The standard current is 110 volts, 60 cycles AC. American-type flat pin plugs are used; adaptors are needed for British and European appliances. There are frequent blackouts *(apagones)* and a torch is useful.

EMBASSIES AND CONSULATES *(embajadas y consulados)*

A large number of countries maintain diplomatic representation, some 46 embassies or consulates in all. Here are some of them:

Canada (Embassy): Capitán Eugenio de Marchena 39, Santo Domingo, tel: 809 685 1136.

France (Embassy): Calle de las Damas 42, Santo Domingo, tel: 809 695 4300.

Germany (Embassy): Lope de Vega 5, Santo Domingo, tel: 809 565 8811.

Haiti (Embassy): Calle Juan Sánchez Ramírez 33, Santo Domingo, tel: 809 686 5778.

Israel (Embassy): Calle Pedro Henríquez Ureña 80, Santo Domingo, tel: 809 541 8974.

Italy (Embassy): Calle Rodríguez Obijo 4, Santo Domingo, tel: 809 682 0830.

Netherlands (Embassy): Calle Max Henríquez Ureña 50, Santo Domingo, tel: 809 262 0320.

Spain (Embassy): Avenida Independencia 1205, Santo Domingo, tel: 809 535 6500.

UK (Embassy): Avenida 27 de Febrero 233, Edificio Corominas Pepín, Santo Domingo, tel: 809 472 7905.

USA (Embassy/Consulate): Calle César Nicolás Pensón, Santo Domingo, tel: 809 221 2171.

EMERGENCIES *(emergencias)* (See also POLICE)

The emergency number for police, fire and ambulance is 911.

G

GAY AND LESBIAN TRAVELLERS

Dominican society is very macho and not tolerant of homosexuality. However, the pink dollar is accepted as yet another facet of tourism, but overt public displays of affection are not recommended. Many hotels, clubs, bars and restaurants are gay friendly and there are several travel agents who specialise in holidays and cruises to the Dominican Republic. The north coast, particularly Cabarete and Sosúa, has plenty going on. Some websites to try include:

www.gaytravel.com   www.outandabout.com
www.gaysports.com   www.outwestadventures.com
www.gayoutdoors.com   www.infohub.com

You can find a travelling companion through www.bluway.com, which also has information on gay-friendly places to stay, and www.debbiesdominicantravel.com which caters for straight as well as gay travellers.

GETTING THERE

Air Travel. There are regular scheduled and charter flights from most European capital cities or connecting flights through Paris or Madrid. From the USA the busiest routes are from Miami and New York, with connecting flights from other US cities. There are also lots of flights from neighbouring islands and Latin American countries. Dominican airlines tend to concentrate on domestic or short hop international flights, but many major international airlines fly to one or more of the country's airports. The flight time from Europe is 8–10 hours, from Toronto 5 hours, New York 3–4 hours, Miami just under 2 hours.

Sea Travel. The only regular passenger service is the 10- to 12-hour car ferry from Puerto Rico, which sails three days a week from Mayagüez to Santo Domingo. Contact Ferries del Caribe, tel: 809 688 4400, www.ferriesdelcaribe.com. Cruise ships call at Santo

Domingo, La Romana and Puerto Plata, allowing a day's sightseeing on land. Cargo ships call from New York, New Orleans, Miami, European and South American countries and you can book a passage for around US$70–130 per person per day. In the UK contact Strand Voyages, Charing Cross Shopping Concourse, The Strand, London WC2N 4HZ, tel: 020-7836 6363. Websites to try include www.travltips.com and www.freightercruises.com.

GUIDES AND TOURS *(guías; visitas guidas)*

There is an official association of registered tour guides: La Asociación de Guías de Turismo de la República Dominicana (Asoguiturd), Vicente C Duarte 3, Santo Domingo, tel: 809 682 0209. It is worth choosing an official guide (who will have a name tag with photo and registration) as they work to an agreed code of conduct with an established pricing system and speak many languages. In Santo Domingo you can find lots of guides outside the cathedral. Rates are negotiable but expect to pay around US$15 for a 2-hour colonial city tour or US$50 for a full day depending on the number of people.

All the resorts have tour agency desks where you can book excursions. These may be on a comfortable coach, a four-wheel-drive vehicle, or even an ex-US military transporter for off-road safaris. The price varies according to distance and length of time involved, but a half-day sightseeing tour will cost US$15–20. If you go on an activity excursion such as scuba diving you can pay US$75–100 for two tanks and maybe lunch. Sailing tours are recommended for a day on the water with snorkelling stops on remote beaches. A catamaran day trip with lunch and open bar will cost around US$60.

HEALTH AND MEDICAL CARE

The most common afflictions for travellers are sunburn, diarrhoea and hangovers. Foreigners are frequently unaware of how little sun they can tolerate before they burn. A high factor sun cream, applied more often than you think necessary, is essential, as is a hat if you are going to be in the sun for long periods, e.g. on a boat. Cooling breezes are deceptive and you can burn even on a cloudy day. Most hotels subscribe to the Cristal programme on food hygiene and the kitchens are checked regularly to make sure that food is prepared correctly and kept at temperatures which will avoid bacteria breeding. When outside the hotel avoid the greasy food cooked at the roadside if you have a sensitive digestion, and always drink plenty of bottled water. Dehydration is common, especially when holiday-makers drink too much alcohol, and can lead to gastric disorders.

At certain times of the year mosquitoes can be a problem and you should take plenty of insect repellent. Malaria is prevalent in Haiti, next door, and in the west of the Dominican Republic in rural, border areas. In 2004, after prolonged rainfall, malaria broke out in the east, around Punta Cana. At the end of the hurricane season, however, it disappeared again. Dengue fever is now more common than malaria and there is no antidote, so it is important to avoid getting bitten.

Large hotels will have their own resident doctor; others will have one on call. 24-hour pharmacies can be found in every town of any size. English speaking doctors can be found in hospitals in Santo Domingo, Puerto Plata, Santiago and Punta Cana, among others.

Always take out travel insurance to cover medical and dental expenses while abroad. Hospitals may refuse to treat you without it. In the case of major emergencies, patients are often flown out to Florida for hospital treatment there.

Where's the nearest (all-night) chemist?	¿Dónde está la farmacia (de guardia) más cercana?
I need a doctor/dentist.	Necesito un médico/dentista.
sunburn/sunstroke	quemadura del sol/una insolación
an upset stomach	mal de estómago

HOLIDAYS *(días festivos)*

The following is a list of national holidays in the Dominican Republic:

1 January	**Año Nuevo**	New Year
6 January	**Día de los Reyes**	Epiphany
21 January	**Día de la Virgen de la Altagracia**	Virgin of Altagracia Day
26 January	**Día de Duarte**	Duarte Day
27 February	**Día de la Independencia**	Independence Day
1 May	**Día de Trabajo**	Labour Day
16 August	**Día de la Restauración**	Restoration Day
24 September	**Día de la Virgen de las Mercedes**	Virgin of Mercy Day
25 December	**Día de la Navidad**	Christmas Day

Movable dates:

Viernes Santo	Good Friday
Corpus Cristi	Corpus Christi

Most of Easter week (Semana Santa) is considered a holiday.

L

LANGUAGE

Spanish is the official language of the Dominican Republic. In tourist areas English, French, German and Italian are widely spoken by people working in tourism, but if you stray off the beaten track a knowledge of Spanish is essential. Pronunciation is Latin American rather than Castillian, but with local idiosyncrasies. The letters 's' and 'd' are often swallowed in the middle of words and this becomes so common that corresponding spelling mistakes are often made, e.g. *despacio* is often written as *depacio*, and *pescado* can be found as *pecao*.

Some typically Dominican vocabulary:

Small boat	**yola**
Motorway, dual carriageway	**autopista**
Slum, cane cutter's hut	**batey**
Thatched hut	**bohío**
Motel rooms with hourly rates	**cabañas**
Family-run grocery store	**colmado**
Dominican cuisine	**comida criolla**
Baseball match	**el play**
Bus, minibus	**guagua**
Motorbike taxi	**motoconcho**
How nice!	**¡qué chulo!**

MAPS

Several free tourist maps are handed out, which are interesting but of little value if you are trying to drive around the island. The best local map publisher is Mapas Gaar, with several town maps as well as their country map, but the style is old-fashioned. Of the foreign maps available the *Insight Fleximap* laminated road map 1:600,000 is very useful, including items of tourist interest and National Parks on the country map and town maps of Santo Domingo, Santiago and Puerto Plata. In 2007, National Geographic published a Dominican Republic map in their waterproof Adventure Map series.

MEDIA

The country is well served for newspapers, boasting several dailies as well as foreign editions of US newspapers such as the *Miami Herald*. There are more than 170 local radio stations, to which Dominicans listen avidly, both for music and for current affairs discussions. Cable television is available and there are numerous stations, including seven local ones. Latin American soap operas are popular.

MONEY

Currency. The currency is the peso (RD$), divided into 100 centavos. There are notes of 5, 10, 20, 50, 100, 500 and 1,000 pesos and coins of 1, 5, 10, 25 and 50 centavos, 1 peso and 5 pesos, although you hardly ever see the tiny coins.

Currency Exchange. The exchange rate fluctuates and in May 2008 the peso was trading at around RD$34 = US$1. Normal banking hours are 8.30am–4pm Monday–Friday, although some banks in supermarkets or shopping malls stay open later and open on Saturday morning. The Banco de Reservas (Banreservas) at the airport remains open for incoming flights. Banks and *cambios* are the official means of changing money. It is not legal to exchange currency on the street. The US dollar is the best currency to bring as not all banks have a market in sterling or the euro. If in doubt, go to the Banco de Reservas, which will exchange most currencies.

Credit cards. Standard international credit cards are widely accepted. In some small shops and in villages only cash is accepted.

ATMs. Automatic teller machines inside and outside banks are widely available. From them you can draw funds in pesos against your credit card account with a Visa or Mastercard, or other debit card on one

Where's the nearest bank/ currency exchange office?	¿Dónde está el banco/la casa de cambio más cercana?
I want to change some pounds/dollars.	Quiero cambiar libras/dólares.
Do you take travellers' cheques?	¿Acceptan cheques de viajero?
Can I pay with a credit card?	¿Se puede pagar con tarjeta?
How much is that?	¿Cuánto es/Cuánto vale?

of the international networks like Cirrus or Plus, provided you know the personal identification number (PIN). Commission can be up to 5 percent. In small towns the machines often do not work.

Travellers' cheques. Travellers' cheques should be denominated in US dollars, they are accepted in Santo Domingo and tourist areas but are difficult to change elsewhere. You will need to show your passport.

O

OPENING TIMES

Dominicans take a long lunch break and many shops and businesses close between 12.30 and 2.30pm, although supermarkets, major stores and tourist shops remain open. Shops generally open 9am–7pm Monday–Saturday; commercial offices 8.30–5pm Monday–Friday and until midday on Saturday; government offices 7.30am–2.30pm Monday–Friday; banks 8.30am–4pm Monday–Friday. Cafés are often open all day but more upmarket restaurants close between lunch and dinner.

P

POLICE (policía)

There is a police service especially for tourism called Politur. Sometimes their offices are in the National Police Station and sometimes in the Tourist Offices. They are helpful and friendly and all their recruits have completed their *bachillerato* at school so they have a higher level of education than the average policeman. In an emergency call 911 for the police. The national call service for Politur is tel: 809 686 8639, 809 686 8301, toll-free line tel: 1-200-3500.

POST OFFICES (correos)

The postal system is run by the Instituto Postal Dominicano. The mail is very slow and you are recommended to go to a post office rather than a mail box if you want to post a letter. *Entrega especial* costs a little more, but is more reliable than the ordinary mail, which sometimes fails to arrive, and if you have anything valuable to send, use a courier service.

PUBLIC TRANSPORT *(transporte publico)*

Buses *(guaguas)*. The country is well served by a network of buses offering long distance or regional routes. There is no central bus station in Santo Domingo or Santiago, each company maintains its own terminal, but in other towns all buses go to the same bus station. The main companies for long distance services are Caribe Tours, Avenida 27 de Febrero esquina Leopoldo Navarro, Santo Domingo, tel: 809 221 4422, and Metro Expreso, Calle Hatuey esquina Avenida Winston Churchill, near 27 de Febrero, Santo Domingo, tel: 809 566 7126. They operate comfortable, air-conditioned buses with videos on board, and are punctual and efficient. There are other bus companies concentrating on regional services, and these are often cheaper but less comfortable. Caribe Tours and Terrabús, Plaza Criolla, Anacaona 15, Santo Domingo, tel: 809 472 1080, operate the route from Santo Domingo to Port-au-Prince in Haiti. On shorter routes between towns there are lots of minibuses *(guaguas)* or cars *(carro público)* which leave when full. These can be very crowded and uncomfortable if you have luggage, but everyone is very friendly and helpful.

In Santo Domingo, the state-run OMSA large buses (RD$10) operate on the main routes into the city, while private bus companies cover the main corridors as well as intersecting routes. You pay per route, so you can travel 25km (16 miles) on the same bus and pay only 10 pesos, but if you change buses you have to pay a further fare of 10 pesos. There are also *públicos*, sometimes called *conchos*, crammed to overflowing, which cost a little more.

Train. A new metro, a rapid transit system, is being built to ease traffic congestion in Santo Domingo. The first of six lines was in-

Where is the (nearest) bus stop?	¿Dónde está la parada de guaguas (más cercana)?
When is the next bus for...?	¿A qué hora sale el próximo guagua para...?
I want a ticket to...	Quiero un billete para...
single (one-way)	ida
return (round-trip)	ida y vuelta
Will you tell me when to get off?	¿Podría indicarme cuándo tengo que bajar?

augurated in 2008. It has 16 stations, 10 of which are underground, and runs for 14.5km (9 miles) from Villa Mella in the north to La Feria in the south of the city.

Taxi. A radio taxi is likely to be more comfortable and safer than a taxi hailed in the street. Short journeys in the capital cost around US$4–5. If a *público* is empty you can hire it for your sole use and it becomes a *carrera*. Motorcycle taxis *(motoconchos)* are the cheapest, at less than US$1 for a local journey (double at night), but despite being fun they are unsafe. The driver must wear a helmet by law, but there is no minimum standard of headgear and they wear all sorts of unsuitable hats. There is no rule for passengers and head injuries are common in accidents. In Samaná motorcycles pull little carts like rickshaws.

Air. Several domestic airlines have services all over the country and offer charter flights to other islands. Air Santo Domingo, Avenida 27 de Febrero 272, Santo Domingo, tel: 809 683 8006, has flights from Santo Domingo to Puerto Plata, Punta Cana, Arroyo Barril and El Portillo, Samaná, as well as from Puerto Plata to Punta Cana. Aerodomca, Aeropuerto la Isabela, Santo Domingo, tel: 809 826 4141, www.aerodomca.com flies to all cities on demand and daily to El Portillo, Samaná. Reserve 24 hours in advance, US$75 one way.

R

RELIGION *(religión; servicios religiosos)*

The majority of Dominicans are Roman Catholic. There are Catholic churches in every town, with patron saints whose feast days *(fiestas patronales)* are celebrated annually with great fanfare, processions and parties. Many Dominicans who never bother to go to Sunday Mass take part in these fiestas. There is also *vodú dominicano*, a syncretic mix of African and European religion loosely based on Catholicism and taking in the *lúas*, or gods, of the African slaves in former times. Although closely related to Haitian voodoo, it probably developed alongside voodoo rather than being an offshoot. There is also a tendency to incorporate supposed Taíno rituals and witchcraft, and a fascination with the supernatural. In island markets you can find stalls called *botánicas*, which sell religious items of all sorts.

T

TELEPHONE *(teléfonos)*

The country code is 809. In 2005, the Dominican Republic switched to a 10-digit telephone system. So all local calls now use the 809 code as part of the number, while calls to other cities or towns begin with the prefix 1 809. Calls coming from overseas remain the same. Phone services are operated by Verizon (formerly Codetel) or Tricom, who maintain offices in most towns (open 8am–10pm), where you can make domestic and international calls, send faxes and sometimes e-mails. Calls are cheaper than in hotels, where there will be a surcharge. There are also payphones for which you need 25-centavo coins. Pre-paid calling cards are available. You can also rent cellular phones.

Can you get me this number? **¿Puede comunicarme con este número?**

TIME ZONES

The Dominican Republic is on Atlantic Standard Time, 4 hours behind GMT.

New York	DR	London	Sydney	Wellington
11am	**noon**	4pm	2am	4am

TIPPING *(propina; servicio)*

Hotel and restaurant bills normally include tax and 10 percent service, but an additional 10 percent is often expected. Hotel porters usually receive US$1 per bag. Hotel maids receive a discretionary tip of perhaps US$1 per day. You do not need to tip taxi drivers, *públicos* or garage attendants.

Is service (tip) included?   **¿Está incluído el servicio?**

TOILETS

Public toilets are few and far between in the Dominican Republic and not particularly nice when you find one. The best place to find a clean toilet is in a large hotel where they are usually located near the reception desk. Alternatively a restaurant may have them, although *comedores* do not always have facilities available. If you go into a bar to find a toilet it would be polite to order a drink while you are there.

Where are the toilets?   **¿Dónde están los servicios?**

TOURIST INFORMATION *(oficinas de información turística)*

The Dominican Republic maintains several tourist offices overseas, including:

Canada: 2080 Rue Crescent, Montréal, Québec, H3G 2B8, tel: 514-4991918. 6 Wellington Street East, Suite 201, Toronto, Ontario, M5E 1S2, tel: 416-3612126.
France: 11 Rue Boudreau, 75009 Paris, tel: 1-4312-9191.
Germany: Hochstrasse 54, 60313 Frankfurt, tel: 069-9139-7878.
Italy: 25 Piazza Castello, 20121 Milan, tel: 02-8057781.
Spain: Calle General Yague 4, Puerta 12, 28020 Madrid, tel: 91-4177375.
UK: 18–21 Hand Court, High Holborn, London WC1V 6JF, tel: 020-7242-7778.
USA: 136 E 57th Street, Suite 803, New York, NY10022, tel: 212-5881012. 848 Brickell Avenue, Suite 405, Miami, Florida 33126, tel: 305-3582899. 561 West Diversey, Suite 214, Chicago, Illinois 60614-1643, tel: 773-5291336.

Where is the tourist office? **¿Dónde está la oficina de turismo?**

There are tourist offices in most towns of any size which attract tourism and kiosks at international airports. In Santo Domingo, there is a tourist office on Plaza Colón in the Palacio Borgella on Isabel la Católica, tel: 809 686 3858. They have lots of leaflets and maps and can help with any information needed. On the street you can ask Politur, the tourism police, for help and advice. The National Tourism Guide is called *La Cótica*. There is a useful tourism telephone directory, *Guía Turística*, available in hotel rooms, which has tourist information at the front, www.paginasamarillas.com.do. The National Hotel and Restaurant Association (Asonahores) and the Tourism Promotion Council publish a *Vacation Planner* which has background information and details on the large hotels. In addition there are regional and town magazines such as *Aquí Santo Domingo*, published bimonthly, which has articles of interest and information on restaurants.

W

WEBSITES AND INTERNET CAFÉS

Websites

There are lots of websites to help you get information before you travel. They include:

www.godominicanrepublic.com the Ministry of Tourism

www.serex.gov.do the Ministry of Foreign Relations

www.dr1.com a news and information website

www.drpure.com concentrates on adventure tourism

Internet Cafés

Verizon is trying to install computer terminals for internet access in all its call centres around the country but they do not always work. They are usually the cheapest service at US$0.75 for 15 minutes, US$1.25 for 30 minutes and US$2 for one hour. There are internet cafés in tourist areas and hotels often offer a service, sometimes free, sometimes reasonable, sometimes extortionate.

In Santo Domingo, the Hodelpa Hotel has internet access at US$5 per hour or US$3 for 30 minutes, while the Herall internet café on Calle El Conde charges US$2 for 1 hour or US$1 for 30 minutes.

In Bávaro, hotels will charge up to US$5 for 30 minutes but if you go into the market at Bibijagua it is much cheaper.

In Cabarete, Telecabarete (open 8am–11pm) charges 2 pesos per minute (minimum 15 minutes), as also does the Internet Gallery. Internet cafés such as these also offer the use of printers, scanners, USB readers, CD burners and international phone calls; the former at US$0.75 per minute to Europe, US$0.25 to the USA and Canada, and the latter at US$0.75 per minute to Europe, US$0.50 to the USA and Canada, minimum two minutes.

In the shopping centre in Playa Dorada, tour agencies offer free internet service if you take one of their tours, otherwise it is US$2 for half an hour (US$1.50 in a hotel).

Recommended Hotels

Hotel construction has boomed since the 1980s, mostly with beach resorts around the coast. Recently, however, there has been a trend for renovating old colonial buildings in Santo Domingo to convert them into boutique hotels, and these are pleasant places to stay if you want a few days in the capital. There are fewer opportunities in the mountains, but even there new hotels are springing up, largely used for weekend breaks by people from the capital.

High season is mid-December to mid-April, with a peak at Christmas and Easter. Holy Week is the main holiday season for Dominicans, so book early to avoid disappointment. In some areas you can find a shoulder season. In Cabarete this is because of good conditions for windsurfing in the autumn when demand is high.

Room price guidelines below are for a double room with bath in high–low season. Always ask if tax and service (total 22 percent) are included. All hotels accept major credit cards. For making reservations the country code is 809.

$$$$	above US$100
$$$	US$60–100
$$	US$30–60
$	below US$30

SANTO DOMINGO

COLONIAL ZONE

Aída $–$$ *El Conde 464 esquina Espaillat, tel: 809 685 7692, fax: 809 688 9350.* This family-run hotel is cheap and cheerful, popular as a good low budget option and conveniently located on the pedestrian shopping street above a shop. Some rooms sleep three. Those with air conditioning don't have opening windows, while those with a balcony have only a fan. No food available. No smoking.

Conde de Peñalba $$–$$$ *El Conde esquina Arzobispo Meriño, tel: 809 6887121, fax: 809 688 7375, www.condepenalba.com.*

Right on the corner of the Plaza Colón, with a popular restaurant and seating outdoors on the square. The rooms upstairs vary. The cheapest are small, windowless and a bit stuffy; the most expensive overlooks the junction with a balcony for people watching, and is great value. All have pleasant furnishings, good new bathrooms, TV, fridge, and phone. No meals are included.

Hodelpa Caribe Colonial $$$–$$$$ *Isabel la Católica 159, tel: 809 688 7799, fax: 809 685 8128, www.hodelpa.com.* From small, standard rooms to superior, superior de luxe and honeymoon suites on the roof, you get what you pay for in terms of space and view, but all have TV, phone, and fridge. There is a small restaurant and bar on the ground floor and a sun deck on the top floor between the suites, which have a great view over the city. Drapes are everywhere, over the beds and even down the stairwell, aiming for an art deco style.

Mercure Comercial Santo Domingo $$$ *El Conde esquina Hostos, tel: 809 688 5500, fax: 809 688 5522, www.accorhotels.com.* Excellent location in the heart of the city, run by the French company, Accor. The reception is through the restaurant/café and there is a lift up to the rooms (probably the only hotel in the old city to have a lift). 96 rooms, not large but well-equipped with L-shaped desk area, internet connection, fridge, TV, good bathrooms; all in orange and beige, not to everyone's taste. French food is served in the brasserie, open breakfast to dinner.

Nicolás de Ovando $$$$ *Calle Las Damas, tel: 809 685 9955, www.accorhotels.com.* The height of luxury in an elegant conversion of the old Casa de Ovando, with heavy stone walls and dark wooden ceilings. 104 rooms and suites with every facility for business or leisure travellers and the ultimate in indulgent bathrooms. A fine courtyard restaurant and views over the river.

Nicolás Nader $$–$$$ *Duarte esquina General Luperón, tel: 809 687 6674, www.naderenterprises.com/hostal.* Another colonial mansion, with nine rooms, all beautifully furnished. The service is friendly and the atmosphere is pleasant. Popular bar with live music at weekends. The feature of this hotel is the modern art decorating every available wall space, which is all for sale. The family that owns the hotel also runs the best art galleries in the Dominican Republic; the Santo Domingo gallery is on Rafael Augusto Sánchez 22.

Saint Amad $$ *Arzobispo Meriño 353 esquina Emiliano Tejera, tel: 809 687 1447, fax: 809 687 1478.* A hotel and restaurant in a recently converted, 300-year-old house. This is great value in an excellent location. The rooms are not large but they are well furnished, with new bathroom fittings, TV, room service, fax and internet connection. The reception is upstairs in front of a charming interior garden. The restaurant downstairs is elegant and pleasant, not cheap, serving international cuisine, seafood, meat and pasta.

Sofitel Francés $$$–$$$$ *Las Mercedes esquina Arzobispo Meriño, tel: 809 685 9331, fax: 809 685 1289, www.accorhotels.com.* 19 luxury rooms in a delightfully restored colonial mansion built in the traditional style around a beautiful courtyard. French run (by Sofitel), with wonderful French food served by the fountain or indoors, this is rather special.

GAZCUE

Casona Dorada $$ *Avenida Independencia 255, tel: 809 221 3535, fax: 809 221 3622, http://lacasonadorada.es.tripod.com.* Rather small, basic rooms with overdone floral décor, but the price includes taxes and some rooms will sleep three. The bathrooms are satisfactory and a good size, and you get air conditioning, TV, fridge, a murky swimming pool and some exercise equipment. Breakfast is US$3.50. Convenient for the Malecón if you want to be in this area.

Courtyard by Marriott $$$ *Avenida Máximo Gómez 50-A, tel: 809 685 1010, fax: 809 685 2003, www.marriott.com/SDQCY.* Opened in 2003 with lots of facilities for business travellers as well as special rates for weekenders, good value rooms sleep up to four comfortably, with some for wheelchair users. Very high standard and friendly atmosphere.

Duque de Wellington $$ *Avenida Independencia 304, tel: 809 682 4525, fax: 809 688 2844, www.hotelduque.com.* The best choice of budget hotels hereabouts. 28 adequate rooms with one or two beds, TV, fridge, room safe box. There is a bar and restaurant if you don't want to eat out.

THE SOUTHEAST

BAYAHIBE

Boca Yate $$ *Avenida Eladia Bayahibe, tel: 809 688 6822, email: h_bocayate@hotmail.com.* French-owned and priced in euros with high season in December–February and August. Rooms around small garden, spacious and comfortable, painted a variety of colours. Seafood restaurant, meal plans available. Day passes to the all-inclusive hotels the other side of the road can be arranged for convenient access to the beach and watersports.

Llave del Mar $ *tel: 809 833 0081.* A basic hotel, opened in 2001, on the main street close to dive shops and restaurants. 25 rooms with fan; those upstairs have a balcony and air conditioning and cost more. Some have a fridge and all have a TV. Good pine furniture and everything perfectly acceptable for the price, but there is no hot water.

Villa Iguana $$ *tel: 809 833 0203, www.villaiguana.de.* Centrally located and unmistakable with its pink concrete walls and thatched balconies. Under German management and offering dive packages and excursions. There are 7 double rooms, some with fan, others with air conditioning, and 3 apartments including a penthouse with a pool. Complimentary internet access and bicycles.

PUNTA CANA

Tortuga Bay $$$$ *tel: 809 959 2262, www.puntacana.com.* The height of luxury at this small villa development designed by Oscar de la Renta alongside the sister resort of Punta Cana. All the facilities of the large resort are available, plus the golf course and marina, but you also have peace and quiet and immaculate service on a pleasant stretch of beach. Your wish is their command and staff are happy to provide whatever you want. Personal transfers from (and to) the airport mean you can be in your room minutes after you land. Bicycles, kayaks and golf carts are provided and the food at the Bamboo restaurant is excellent .

MICHES

La Loma $–$$ *tel: 809 558 5562, fax: 809 553 5564, www.punta elrey.com/seiten/e-uebern-hotel-laloma.html.* Perched on top of a hill overlooking a huge sweep of coastline, this hotel can be sold on its view alone. There are eight rooms and one three-bedroom suite, all with simple pine furniture and a pleasant blue and yellow décor. All rooms have a large balcony, a double and a single bed, some have air conditioning, all have TV and hot water. Feast your eyes on the view while eating in the restaurant. There is also a small pool. The main drawback is access, along extremely poor roads. The unspoilt beach of Playa Esmeralda is just along the coast, where sister hotel Punta El Rey Beach Club offers bungalows by the sea and the Coco Loco restaurant.

THE SOUTHWEST

BAORUCO

Aparta Hotel Pontevedra $$–$$$ *tel: 809 341 8462, www. pontevedracaribe.com.* 16 simple yet comfortable suites with cooking facilities, on the seafront with a pool, restaurant and bar. Very popular with Dominicans from the capital so advance reservation at weekends is essential.

Casa Bonita $$$$ *Carretera de la Costa, km16, Barahona, tel: 809 696 0215, fax: 809 223 0548, www.casabonitadr.com.* Up on a hill, the hotel has a lovely view of the sea, particularly from the thatched restaurant and lounge, which have no walls. The pleasant aspect, gardens and small pool make the hotel a very relaxing and romantic place, and there are great opportunities for exploring the nearby

Sierra de Baoruco. The 12 rooms are stylishly decorated, with beautiful arty photographs by Eladio Fernández on the walls. Definitely the nicest place to stay in the area.

THE INTERIOR

CONSTANZA

Alto Cerro $–$$ *tel: 809 696 0202, fax: 809 530 6193, email: c.matias@verizon.net.do.* Light and airy hotel with a spectacular view across the farming valley. Rooms or villas with two to three bedrooms sleeping up to seven, all with balconies. Villas have open plan kitchen/dining/living room with tiled floors, pine furniture, TV, phone, fireplace and wall safe. There are pretty flowers all around and a large, grassy playground with swings and seesaws. Camping can be arranged. There is a small grocery shop beside the reception for booze, canned foods and essentials. The restaurant upstairs has seating inside or out on the balcony. They raise their own geese, guinea fowl, rabbits, turkeys and fruit and flowers. The fruit is grown without the use of chemicals. Quad bikes and horses are for hire.

Hotel Rancho Constanza & Cabañas de la Montana $$ *Calle San Francisco de Macorís 99, Sector Don Bosco, tel: 809 682 2410/539 3268.* This alpine-style hotel was new in 2002 and has 12 large rooms with a great view across the valley, good big bathrooms, TV, and tiled floors, and some have kitchenettes. The 15 cabins can each sleep a family of six but are dark and basic with walls which don't reach the ceilings. The kitchens are adequate but there is a restaurant in the hotel if you don't want to cook. Outside there is a volleyball/basketball court, billiards and a children's playground.

JARABACOA

Gran Jimenoa $$ *Avenida La Confluencia, Los Corralitos, tel: 809 574 6304, fax: 809 574 4177, www.granjimenoa.com.* A few kilometres outside town down a dirt road, this 28-room hotel has a very special location in lush greenery right beside the river. When the water level is low you can bathe in the *balneario* between the boulders, otherwise head for the pool and Jacuzzi. The restaurant overlooks the Jimenoa and a footbridge leads to the karaoke lounge on the other side, where weddings and parties are held. You can see herons and other water birds fishing. The rooms have one or two beds, TV, phone and room service. There are indoor games such as ping pong, billiards and dominoes. Local meats are served in the restaurant: guinea fowl, goat, rabbit, *carne salada*, as well as more standard fare. Packed at weekends but quiet mid-week. Excursions are available.

Rancho Baiguate $$ *tel: 809 574 6890, fax: 809 574 4940, www. ranchobaiguate.com.* Priced per person including breakfast, lunch and dinner and all taxes. The centre for adventure sports in the area, this is also a great place to relax in the country. Rooms vary from standard to luxury but are all spacious and rustic. There is no TV, phone or air conditioning, just peace and quiet and animal noises. You can choose from a range of sports: rafting, canyoning, tubing, hang gliding, horse riding, quad bikes, mountain biking and hiking Pico Duarte, with a team of very fit, experienced, multilingual guides. There is also a swimming pool, indoor sports and an adventure playground for adults, Maroma's Parcours, where a keen sense of balance is required to negotiate logs suspended by chains, swings, tightropes, etc.

THE NORTH COAST

MONTE CRISTI

Cayo Arena $$–$$$ *Playa Juan de Bolaños, tel: 809 579 3145, fax: 809 579 2096, www.cayoarena.com.* This is an aparthotel on the other side of the road from the sea, with a small pool, restaurant and bar outside and lots of well-established tropical plants around the parking area. The apartments have two bedrooms and sleep four, air conditioning in one room, a fan in the other. There is a large living area with French doors to a small balcony, but no TV. The kitchen has a gas hob and cooker and is adequate, but the bathroom is basic, no frills. Excursions arranged. The beach is not great and the salt pans are to the rear.

Los Jardines $ *Playa Juan de Bolaños, tel: 809 579 2091, www.el bistro.com.* Set in immaculate gardens, this small lot contains two bungalows with two rooms each. They are very simple but the bathrooms are good. The sea is to the front and the salt flats are at the back. No food is available at the bungalows and there are no cooking facilities, but El Bistrot restaurant in town is under the same ownership *(see page 140)*. The owner, Hervé, runs boat trips to the Cayos Siete Hermanos and excursions to the Citadelle in Haiti.

PUERTO PLATA

Castilla $ *José del Carmen Ariza 34, tel: 809 586 7267, email: samsbar@gmail.com.* There are not many options in the town because of the hotel development on the beaches at Playa Dorada and at Cofresí. Hotel Castilla was the first hotel here, dating from the 1890s, and has a quaint historic charm. On the ground floor is Sam's Bar and Grill, named after a former resident Bassett hound. Rooms are very basic with thin walls and have private or shared bathroom, but it is very cheap. Long term rates are available.

PLAYA DORADA

Gran Ventana $$$ *PO Box 22, Puerto Plata, tel: 809 320 2111, fax: 809 320 2112, www.victoriahoteles.com.do.* Nice, all-inclusive hotel offering something for everybody. One wing is quiet, designed for older couples who want to read and relax, while the central area around the main pool is for families and young couples. A la carte meals are on offer as well as good buffet food. The 506-room hotel is right on the beach but only a short walk to the Centro Comercial if you want to go shopping or to the movies. The hotel is family-owned: Don Isidro is a local cattle rancher and his daughter, an architect, designed their three hotels: Gran Ventana, La Victoria and the new Casa Colonial. La Victoria is more upmarket, quieter and aimed at golfers as it is right by the club house with a tremendous view over the course and lakes and up to Mt Isabela de Torres. Casa Colonial is a 5-star, all-suite hotel, small, intimate, with a state-of-the-art spa, the most luxurious beach hotel in the country.

SOSÚA

Casa Valeria $$ *Dr Rosen 28, tel: 809 571 3565, www.hotelcasa valeria.com.* Small, pleasant and quiet, one of the nicer budget options in town. A short walk from the beach the hotel is secluded in trees, with its nine rooms and studios, pool, restaurant and bar. The service is friendly and helpful. Dutch-run.

Piergiorgio Palace $$$ *tel: 809 571 2626, fax: 809 571 2786, www.piergiorgiopalace.com.* A landmark hotel perched on the promontory at the end of the bay on the cliffs overlooking crystal clear water. There is no beach but steps lead down to the sea where the snorkelling is great along the rocks. There is also a small, clean pool for safer bathing. In Victorian style, the hotel is very elegant, with impeccable décor, clean and bright with tiled floors and a stylish floral design in the bedrooms. All have a semi-circular balcony and excellent bathrooms with lots of goodies and big shower heads. In addition there are two penthouses with every luxury.

CABARETE

Velero Beach Resort $$$–$$$$ *Calle La Punta 1, tel: 809 571 9727, fax: 809 571 9722, www.velerobeach.com.* This new, 4-star hotel is built at the east end of Cabarete beach around neat, manicured lawns and palm trees going down to the beach. Despite being top of the range, the rooms are good value for money, having a great view, patio or balcony with mosquito screens at the French doors, solid wooden furniture, attractive décor and excellent bathrooms, all the height of luxury. A room and a suite can connect to make a family apartment with a full kitchen. There is only a beach bar, no restaurant, but there is an Italian restaurant just behind the entrance to the hotel, and it's a short walk along the beach to get to others.

Villa Taína $$–$$$ *Calle Principal, tel: 809 571 0722, fax: 809 571 0883, www.villataina.com.* The reception is on the main street in the heart of the town, but you walk through to a separate block to get to the rooms, which are right on the beach and peaceful. There is a variety of good-sized rooms, some with kitchenette and penthouse rooms. Breakfast at the restaurant on the sand is included, as are beach chairs and towels, and one hour's use of boogie boards. Windsurfing instruction and equipment hire is right beside the hotel. There is a small pool if the sea is too rough but most people sunbathe on the deep expanse of beach or seek the shade of the palm trees. An excellent location for all facilities, friendly and helpful staff, gay-friendly.

RÍO SAN JUAN

Bahía Blanca $–$$ *Calle Gastón F Deligne 5, tel: 809 589 2563, fax: 809 589 2528.* 20 simple rooms with one or two beds, fan and hot water in the shower, all opening onto a shared veranda with a fabulous view of the bay and the north coast – wonderful at sunset. The hotel is perched on a cliff with a beach either side and the water below is an array of colours, with reef, sand and sea grass. The restaurant, in a cool green and white, has the same view and is a pleasant place to sit and enjoy food and vista. Meal plans are recommended as there is not much to choose from locally. A dive shop is just up the road, as is the Laguna Gri Grí for boat trips in the mangroves.

SAMANÁ PENINSULA

SAMANÁ

Bahía View $–$$ *Av Circunvalación 4, tel: 809 538 2186, email: asavachao@aol.com.* Simple accommodation in a convenient location in town overlooking the bay. Nine rooms with air conditioning and fan, some with balconies, of different sizes sleeping up to eight people. Restaurant on the first floor.

Docia $ *tel: 809 538 2041.* Just above La Churcha with a good view of the bay either side of the church, this is a very simple, but clean and new guest house with 15 rooms. The eight rooms upstairs are newer and better equipped than those downstairs and it is worth paying the extra US$2–3 for the big windows, light and airy rooms and new bathrooms. All very basic, no frills but cheap. Fan, hot water, one or two beds.

LAS GALERAS

Villa Serena $$$$ *tel: 809 583 0000, www.villaserena.com.* One of the loveliest hotels in the country. Plantation house style buildings in picture-book location by the sea looking out to a desert island with coconut palms on it. Wooden balconies and verandas, overhanging roofs and a grand staircase leading down from reception to the elegant gardens complete the picture. European menu in the restaurant, good food in lovely setting.

LAS TERRENAS

Fata Morgana $ *tel: 809 836 5541, email: editdejong@hotmail.com.* This clean and pleasant hostel is popular with backpackers and those on a tight budget. It is away from the beach but not far from the main road. Rooms sleep from one to four people, with bathroom, terrace, laundry service and book exchange. Long stays are welcomed. To get there, turn down Fabio Abreu, then turn right down a track which leads to the French school; just before the school take a track to your left.

Kanesh Beach 'Las Cayenas' $$ *tel: 809 240 6080, fax: 809 240 6177, www.lascayenas.com.* A small Swiss-run hotel in a perfect location across the track from the beach and surrounded by coconut palms. Breakfast is included, served on the veranda. There is an independent German-run restaurant and bar in the garden if you don't want to walk far to eat. The rooms are simple, with or without a balcony, and the bathrooms are fine. Mini golf and ping pong for entertainment.

Las Palmas $$ *Calle El Portillo, tel: 809 240 6436, fax: 809 240 6435, www.vamosalaspalmas.com.* 23 villas sleep four in two bedrooms (one upstairs) with living room, two bathrooms and verandah, cable TV, fridge, hob, kitchen utensils. Rooms are cleaned twice a week. A very pretty development, painted blue and yellow and set in attractive flower gardens and palm trees just across the track from the beach. Monthly rates available if you can't tear yourself away.

Recommended Restaurants

In the large towns and on the north coast there are numerous restaurants of all types serving good food at reasonable prices. Many hotel restaurants are also worth trying; some are of gourmet standard. In the smaller towns and along the main roads you will find family-run cafés serving Dominican food, called *comedores*. A full meal in a *comedor* should cost no more than US$3–4 outside the capital, although in Santo Domingo prices are higher at around US$4–6. There are also more upmarket restaurants specialising in Dominican food, often in rustic surroundings, which will charge the same as a regular restaurant.

Dominicans are keen on fried or roast chicken (*pollo al carbón*) and there are plenty of fast food places, both local and the American chains for burgers, chicken and pizzas.

The prices indicated are for a three-course meal per person without drinks and excluding tax and service. Beer can cost around US$1–3 for a small bottle, depending on the location, and rum is also cheap, but wine can be expensive and is not generally well cared for, except in the very top restaurants.

$$$$$	above US$35
$$$$	US$20–35
$$	US$10–20
$	below US$10

SANTO DOMINGO

El Conuco $$ *Casimiro de Moya 152 esquina José Joaquín Pérez, tel: 809 686 0129. Open for lunch and dinner.* Quite a touristy place with lunchtime buffet set up for tour parties, but popular nonetheless and you will find Dominicans eating here. The restaurant is decorated like a thatched barn and serves up typical Dominican dishes such as *sancocho, chivo guisado* and *la bandera Dominicana*. The cooking is good, the portions large and the service friendly and efficient. National dance displays are usually performed at lunchtime and there is music in the evenings.

La Briciola $$$ *Arzobispo Meriño 152, tel: 809 688 5055, www.labriciola.com.do. Open for lunch and dinner.* The restaurant is in the lovely courtyard of a colonial mansion and a delightfully romantic place to dine, with an Italian menu.

Lumi's Park $$ *Avenida Abraham Lincoln 809, tel: 809 540 4755, 5404584 for delivery, email: lumis.park@codetel.net.do. Open daily for lunch and dinner until dawn.* Dominican cooking, always full and popular but if you can't get a table you can order take-away, or even home delivery service. Dining is outdoors, under canvas, and you can indulge in a huge *churrasco* or try *mofongo*, a hearty stew with plantains.

Mesón de la Cava $$$$ *Avenida Mirador del Sur 1, tel: 809 533 2818, email: pescador@codetel.net.do. Open daily for lunch and dinner.* In the unusual setting of a cave, this is an atmospheric place to dine, elegant and expensive with international menu, good seafood and extensive wine list.

Museo de Jamón $$–$$$ *Las Atarazanas 17, tel: 809 688 9644. Open daily for lunch and dinner.* One of several restaurants here in Las Atarazanas, converted dock workshops from colonial days. This one is Spanish and specialises in tapas. Numerous hams hang from the ceiling, giving the restaurant its name.

THE SOUTHEAST

BOCA CHICA

Neptuno's Club Restaurant $$$–$$ *tel: 809 523 4703, fax: 809 523 4251. Open daily for lunch and dinner.* On the waterfront beside the Coral Hamaca hotel, the restaurant juts out over the water, with the bar located in a replica of the *Santa María*, Columbus' caravelle. Seafood is the house speciality, but meat dishes and a children's menu are available. A shark tank and aquarium provide interest and there is added entertainment with live music on Wednesday and Saturday night. If you don't fancy this romantic setting, home delivery is offered within Boca Chica.

BAVARO

Capitán Cook $$ *Playa Cortecito, tel: 809 552 0646. Open daily for lunch and dinner until midnight.* On the sand under trees for shade, a great escape from all-inclusive hotels, serving fresh shrimp, lobster and fish straight from the fishing boats. Always full, very popular and deservedly so. Great food and atmosphere.

THE INTERIOR

CONSTANZA

Antojitos d'Lauren $ *Duarte 17. Open daily for breakfast, lunch and dinner.* Informal, with plastic tables. Local specialities include *sancocho* and *chuletas* but it is particularly popular at night for pizza, when it comes alive as a family place with dancing.

Comedor Gladys $ *Luperón 36, tel: 809 539 3625. Open daily for breakfast, lunch and dinner.* An unprepossessing *comedor* which serves up an excellent and filling *menú del día* with a choice of meat dishes for US$2.50. If she hasn't got what you want in the canteen, just ask, other things are available. The pastry and cake counter is popular with children coming out of school.

JARABACOA

La Herradura $$ *Independencia esquina Duarte, tel: 809 574 4795. Open daily for lunch and dinner.* One of the best places to eat, with main dishes around US$4–6 and a wide choice including pasta, meat, fish, sandwiches and salads. Decorated in ranch style to reflect the owner's love of horses and cowboys. Live music weekend evenings.

Rancho Restaurant $$–$$$ *On the main road opposite the Esso station, tel: 809 574 4557. Open for lunch and dinner.* A dark but cosy restaurant which is part of the Rancho Baiguate group and well-frequented by the hotel guests as well as locals. The food is good, with creole and international dishes on the menu and locally grown ingredients. Works of local artists displayed on the walls.

Vistabella Club Bar & Grill $–$$ *Just off the road to Salto Jimenoa, 5km from town. Open for lunch and dinner.* Part of the Rancho Baiguate group and often used at night by guests of the hotel, but nicer during the day when you can see the view across the valley. On the menu are guinea fowl, goat, rabbit, sausage and other local delicacies such as *casabe con ajo*, garlic cassava bread.

THE NORTH COAST

MONTE CRISTI

Comedor Adela $ *Juan de la Cruz Álvarez 41, tel: 809 579 2254. Open daily for lunch and dinner.* Excellent spicy goat stew and other meat dishes with the usual rice, beans and salad, all nicely presented, filling and cheap. Eat indoors or outside in the patio.

El Bistrot $$ *San Fernando 26, tel: 809 579 2091. Open Mon–Fri 11am–2.30pm, 6pm–midnight, Sat–Sun 10am–midnight, www.el bistro.com.* Set in a lovely courtyard with big wooden doors off the road. The bar has white furniture with rocking chairs, and the seating for the restaurant is outside in the patio or under cover. A wide range of food on the menu – sandwiches, salads, pastas, grill, seafood, fish and meat.

PUERTO PLATA

La Parrillada Steak House $–$$ *Avenida Manolo Tavarez Justo, tel: 809 586 1401. Open for lunch and dinner.* Outdoor seating, but despite being near a busy road the traffic is not too noisy. Come here for good Argentine steak, the *churrasco* is very tasty and the portions are generous.

Sam's Bar & Grill $–$$ *José del Carmen Ariza 34, tel: 809 586 7267, www.samsbar.tk. Open daily for breakfast, lunch and dinner.* A popular meeting place for a drink and a bite to eat. US-style menu, with great spare ribs as well as some delicious desserts. Rooms are available in the Hotel Castilla if you can't bear to move on, see page 133.

SOSÚA

On the Waterfront $$ *Calle Dr Rosen 1, tel: 809 571 3024, www.hotelwaterfrontdr.com. Open daily for breakfast, lunch and dinner.* Known for its spectacular location on the clifftop overlooking the sea, this is the ideal place to come for sunset watching, with a convenient happy hour from 4–6pm. The food is good too, with outdoor dining and lots of choice: seafood, meat dishes and snacks. In season there is usually an all-you-can-eat barbeque on Friday nights and live music most nights.

CABARETE

Blue Moon $–$$ *Los Brazos, 20 minutes outside town, tel: 809 223 0614, www.bluemoonretreat.net. Open for dinner.* Worth the excursion out of town for the (East) Indian food served on banana leaves. Reservations are essential and it is best if you are in a large group so that you can choose lots of dishes and try a bit of everything.

Comedor Loli $ *Turn off main road at sign for Parque Nacional El Chocó. Open daily for breakfast, lunch and dinner.* This is one of several *comedores* along this road, and a cheap and cheerful change from the international-style places along the seafront. Good, local food, instant service with a choice of many ways of cooking chicken, beef and fish. More seafood is offered at night. Unbelievably good value at less than US$2 for *menú del día*.

SAMANÁ PENINSULA

LAS TERRENAS

Casa Boga $$–$$$ *Casa de los Pescadores, tel: 809 240 6321, email: casaboga@terra.es. Open for lunch and dinner.* The Fishermen's Huts are a collection of wooden shacks on the beach, all converted to restaurants and a lovely place to have dinner with the sea lapping the sand nearby. This is about the best of the bunch, offering excellent Basque cooking. Ask for advice when choosing as there are so many types of fish on offer, which can be cooked in so many ways, all delicious.

INDEX

Berlitz pocket guide
Dominican Republic

Second Edition 2009
Written by Sarah Cameron
Series Editor: Tony Halliday

Photography credits
Luis Gomez Cardenas 39; Glyn Genin 60;
Wolfgang Rössig 48; Martin Thomas 11, 76; Phil
Wood 6, 9, 12, 15, 17, 20, 22, 24, 25, 26, 27, 28,
30, 31, 33, 34, 36, 37, 38, 40, 42, 43, 45, 47, 52,
53, 56, 58, 59, 61, 63, 65, 66, 67, 68, 69, 70, 71,
77, 80, 82, 85, 88, 89, 91, 93, 94, 97, 100;
Dominican Republic Tourist Board 7, 8, 18, 35,
44, 46, 50, 64, 73, 74, 76, 78, 86, 90, 98.

Cover picture: Donald Nausbaum

Every effort has been made to provide
accurate information in this publication,
but changes are inevitable. The publisher
cannot be responsible for any resulting
loss, inconvenience or injury.

All Rights Reserved
© 2009 Berlitz Publishing/Apa
Publications GmbH & Co. Verlag KG,
Singapore Branch, Singapore

Printed in Singapore by Insight Print
Services (Pte) Ltd, 38 Joo Koon Road,
Singapore 628990. Tel: (65) 6865-1600.
Fax: (65) 6861-6438

Berlitz Trademark Reg. U.S. Patent Office
and other countries. Marca Registrada

Contact us

At Berlitz we strive to keep our guides as
accurate and up to date as possible, but if you
find anything that has changed, or if you have
any suggestions on ways to improve this guide,
then we would be delighted to hear from you.

Berlitz Publishing, PO Box 7910,
London SE1 1WE, England.
fax: (44) 20 7403 0290
email: berlitz@apaguide.co.uk
www.berlitzpublishing.com